*"Children are the world's most valuable resource
and its best hope for the future."*

—John F. Kennedy

THAT'S MY BABY

RUTH LOGAN HERNE

Whistle Stop Café Mysteries is a trademark of Guideposts.

Published by Guideposts
100 Reserve Road, Suite E200
Danbury, CT 06810
Guideposts.org

Cover and interior design by Müllerhaus
Cover illustration by Greg Copeland at Illustration Online LLC.
Typeset by Aptara, Inc.

ISBN 978-1-961126-33-6 (hardcover)
ISBN 978-1-961126-34-3 (epub)

Printed and bound in the United States of America
10 9 8 7 6 5 4 3 2 1

THAT'S MY BABY

Kielce, Poland
July 1939

Blessings, my beloved Nessie!

I send to you my greatest creation to date, dear sister. It is packaged well (although shipping can disturb even the most carefully wrapped items), so if you find it is in need of straightening or repair, I know your clever hands will handle the task with the skill required. I have absolute faith in that, for I know you and your dear husband, George, so well.

Joseph works hard these days. His railroad job keeps him busy. The scheduling is not what it once was, but you know my Joseph. He is always ready to put his hand to the task. He is quite willing to work extra hours to help pay for the home and land we love. Our acreage grows well. How insightful of our Baba Amalia to make that purchase so long ago. She was such a clever, giving grandmother!

I use her sewing machine to create things for our-selves and others. Serviceable things, yes, but with a bit of flair, much as our mother used to do. We strive to be a source of comfort to those around us. Our land is lush with the vegetables and foods we've enjoyed all our lives, and the wheat grows as it should. We will harvest on schedule as nature provides, although nature herself follows an individual pattern. Our cousins will help oversee the harvest, as they have for so long.

You must tell me of your life in New York—what it is like, and how different it is from our rural existence here. We hear so much from so many, but I find it hard to separate fact from fiction. I know I will always hear truth from you, even when it is hard to share. I appreciate that, dear sister. I have always looked up to your experience, your wisdom. You understood what many could not admit or believe, and it has made such a dif-ference for you. I am proud of you. I share your news with the rest of the family as it arrives.

Joseph feels as I do—that your wisdom has set a goal for many, including us, Lord willing. Time and politics can keep us apart only for so long, dear sister, and I await the time when we can join hands and laugh once more. For now, I send you my best works via Aunt Berta. Much as Mama trusted her with our childhood education in a land not our own, I trust her help now.

I send God's many blessings to you and yours and cherish the times we've spent together here on the farm. It is not nearly the same without you, and it would be wonderful to see my beloved sister once more!

Ever yours,

Anya

CHAPTER ONE

"I don't like quiet days," Janet Shaw announced as she refilled the refrigerated pastry case with slices of homemade pie Monday afternoon. Chocolate cream. Mississippi mud. And in honor of the coming spring, a fresh lemon meringue.

"For the shortest month, February sure felt long," agreed Debbie Albright, her business partner and lifelong best friend. "But I knew spring was in the air when my buddy came to work wearing a T-shirt and jeans. A choice she's probably regretting now that the outdoor temps have nose-dived back into the thirties. It's the beginning of March, Janet," she teased, smiling. "That's a bit optimistic, even for you."

"Admittedly a bad choice." Janet slanted a wry glance toward the darkening sky. "Ian dropped me off while my car's getting new tires, and I let the warm morning sweep me away. I didn't think to check the forecast." Her husband, Ian, was the chief of police.

Thick clouds hadn't just moved into the area. They'd piled in, dark, ominous, and ready to deliver snow or rain, depending on the temperature. Volatile weather was simply part of their late-winter reality in Dennison, Ohio. While some stalwart crocuses peeked up along walkways, nothing else dared bloom, despite the warming trend they'd enjoyed that morning. With temps in the midthirties now, Janet should have brought a jacket to work. A warm one.

"You'd think I'd know better after over forty years of living here," she groused as Debbie finished cleaning.

"I can give you a lift home, unless you'd rather walk." Debbie gave Janet a wry expression. "It's not exactly T-shirt weather yet. I think we still have a few weeks to wait for that, especially if you're after a walk that boasts a full array of spring flowers." She washed her hands and dried them at the sink. "Are you about ready?"

The back door flew open.

Sadie Flaherty, their childhood friend, stood framed in the doorway. Sadie owned That's My Baby, a doll store that she called "the doll hospital" over in Uhrichsville.

Sadie clutched a quilted bag to her chest. The bag was pretty, done in bright pastels. Obviously, Janet wasn't alone in wishing for spring. Sadie rushed in, clearly distraught, and pushed the door shut behind her.

Janet took a step forward. "Sadie, what's wrong?"

"Can I talk to you?" Sadie whispered, then jerked her head around as if to make sure they were alone. "Both of you?"

"Of course." Debbie motioned toward the nearest table. "What's happened? Are the kids all right? Is Drew?"

"They're fine." Sadie Harper Stone had married Drew Flaherty nearly twenty years before. It had taken them a long time to have kids, and when it had finally happened, they were delighted to find out they were having twins. Middle schoolers Bria and Brooke were avid soccer players and violinists, on the go all the time.

Janet drew out a chair for Sadie, and then she and Debbie sat down.

Sadie sank into the seat and glanced around again.

"No one's here but us," Janet assured her.

"I was checking the windows," she said. "In case anyone followed me."

"Why would anyone follow you?" Debbie asked, clearly concerned.

"*Is* someone following you?" Janet asked. "I can call Ian. He'd be here in a heartbeat."

Sadie's worried expression deepened. "No, but they could be. I can't believe I made such a rookie mistake." Her hands shook, and her breath came quickly. "I know better. I'm not a kid on the internet for the first time. But who'd have thought posting a picture of an old rag doll would create an issue? Not me, certainly, and yet…" She sighed, stuck her hand into the bag on her lap, and then withdrew it slowly. She clutched an old-fashioned rag doll, rudimentary in appearance. Simple rags, tied together to form a semblance of head, body, and limbs—the kind a child might have had on the prairie or during the Great Depression.

"It's this," she told them. She set the rag doll on the table. It didn't appear dirty, but it did smell a little musty. "I found this as I was clearing out Aunt Lena's attic a few days ago. It was in an old trunk."

Debbie picked up the doll and examined it. "It doesn't seem to be anything special. Probably stuffed away a long time from the smell of it."

"That's what I thought," Sadie agreed. "So I snapped a picture of it and posted it to my social media. My followers love to see original creations like this. Depression-era handmade dolls are a good reminder to be grateful for better times."

"I don't see the problem," Debbie said. "Nothing a gentle washing wouldn't cure."

"Except there's this." Sadie hesitated then opened her other hand. On her palm lay a tiny satin bag. It was old-fashioned royal blue satin—nothing polyester about it. When she upended the miniature satchel, a small brooch with a square green stone fell onto her palm.

Eyes wide, Janet bent closer. "Is that a real emerald?"

"It's gorgeous." Debbie whistled softly as she picked up the brooch. "Truly stunning."

"Where did it come from?" Janet asked.

"Her." Sadie touched the doll. "I posted her online and got a fair number of likes and comments, but then this morning an email was in the store's account. Here's what it said." She handed them her phone.

I am tired of secrets. So tired. I was forced to keep them for so long because of your great-grandmother, but she is long gone, and the time for secrets is past. No more, Sadie. I will keep them no more.

That doll had a purpose. A quiet purpose, and there you are, flaunting her on social media, as if she were any old thing.

She's not. Within her folds she held potential. Freedom. Opportunity. And yet we were sworn to silence as if we'd done something wrong.

I'm done.

I will no longer be quiet. At long last, I will let the truth be known. Truth about your family, your ancestors, your children, and mine.

It will alter things. There's nothing to be done about that. Lives will change.

They must.

But that is not my worry. Seeing her was the message I needed.

I will come. Some way, somehow, I will come. And I promise you this: the truth will set us free, as it should have long ago.

M.E.

Janet's jaw dropped. "You know this person?"

"No."

"But that line—" Janet pointed to the message. "'Within her folds she held potential. Freedom. Opportunity.' Does that mean this person knew something was hidden inside a doll that has to be at least fifty years old?"

"Older than that," Sadie said. "I think the doll dates back to World War II. My great-aunt Lena Harper had Gigi living with her after Great-Grandpa passed away. Gigi was my great-grandmother, Annie Harper. Most of Gigi's stuff got moved to Aunt Lena's attic along with the tons of things already up there. There were newspapers in the trunk for packing, I think. To cushion things. They were dated 1950."

"Where were they from?" Janet asked.

"New York City," Sadie said. She paused and took a breath, as if bracing herself. "Finding the doll and the brooch was weird, but that's not what has me upset. My family had secrets."

Janet and Debbie exchanged glances. They'd known Sadie for decades, and she'd never mentioned such a thing to them before.

She lifted a napkin from the rack on the table and twisted it between her fingers. "I've known that for a long time. I don't know what they are, but I know they exist," she continued. "There were whispers and dark looks between the adults when I was small, and sometimes Gigi would get this strange expression on her face. It was more than fear. It was abject terror, as if someone was after her. Aunt Lena called it 'the demons of war,' but there was no explanation about what she meant by that."

She hesitated again, and Janet and Debbie remained silent, waiting for her to continue.

"We weren't allowed to talk about World War II or emigration or even do family research, because Gigi was so sensitive to it. By the time I was old enough to demand answers, my life had gotten busy."

"I hear you," Janet murmured. "Jobs, kids, life. It piles on."

"But now Aunt Lena's gone, and I've inherited what was her home and the business we both loved. Then out of the blue comes some mysterious email." She tapped the *Do Not Reply to This Email* line on the message. "An email talking about secrets, about the doll, about changing lives. It freaked me out."

"I don't blame you," Debbie said.

Sadie sighed. "I don't have anyone to ask about any of this. Dad's gone, and Mom's remarried and living in Florida with her new husband. Aunt Lena was the last of the Harpers who would have remembered anything, and now she's gone too. I'm the one who has to worry about what this person knows about my family. How am I supposed to handle that? Having a random stranger threaten to show up? And how will I even know who he or she is?"

"Did you try answering it?" Debbie asked.

"It says 'do not reply.'" Sadie met Debbie's gaze, puzzled. "So I can't answer it, right?"

"I'd give it a try," Debbie replied. "That line might be to discourage a response, without actually preventing one. Worst-case scenario, your message might go to a vast email wasteland somewhere. Either way, it can't hurt to try, can it?"

"You're right. I'll do that when I get home. Maybe I'll get an answer." Sadie smiled ruefully. "I'm such a rule follower. It said, 'do not reply,' so I didn't. Where has my spirit of adventure gone?"

"It's still there," Janet assured her. "It's just momentarily knocked out." She frowned at the email address. "It's hard to know exactly what the person is thinking from the email, but it's not hard to hear the angst. Would it be okay if Debbie and I dig into this for you and see what we can find? You can let us know if your response gets a reaction."

Sadie nodded. "I was hoping you'd offer. That's why I came to you two. You've got a knack for untying knots, and I'm too close to this to approach it rationally. I thought this was merely Grandma Mary's or Gigi's old doll that got stuffed in an old trunk a long time ago. I don't think I would have ever found the brooch inside without that email."

"You didn't feel it in the doll?" Janet asked.

"Yes, but I thought it was some rubber or stone they built the doll around," Sadie admitted. "From the little I do know, my family came here right after World War II with nothing, so where does an emerald brooch fit in? Is it part of my heritage? Hidden for safekeeping then forgotten? Or something more sinister? What if my ancestors were part of something illegal? And who is this email from?" She indicated the message with a glance toward her phone. "They make it sound as if they know who I am, where my business is, and where I live. But I know nothing about them, their intentions, or how they knew something was hidden in the doll."

"Secrets have a way of working their way to the surface eventually," Janet said.

Sadie grimaced. "I don't know whether I should be comforted by that or not."

"We'll look into it," Janet promised. "Quietly. There may be a perfectly innocent reason—"

"For a pricey brooch to be hidden in a tacky rag doll and some random stranger knowing about it?"

Janet laid her hand over her friend's. "No use borrowing trouble, Sadie. We'll see what we can find. In the meantime, do you want to keep the brooch in the safe at my house? I can promise it'll be secure there."

Relief covered her friend's features. "Yes please."

"And how should she handle the anonymous message sender?" Debbie mused as Janet slid the tiny satin bag into her pocket. "This person obviously follows Sadie's social media. Are they expecting a reaction?"

"They might be expecting it, but that doesn't mean we give them the satisfaction of one," Janet said. "My advice is to ignore it, at least in public. Continue your normal day-to-day posts as if you never received this email."

Sadie nodded, seeming calmer already.

"I think that's good advice," said Debbie. "Do you have any old family pictures, Sadie? From World War II or before?"

Sadie thought for a moment before answering. "Mom might have had some. If she did, they'd be up in our attic. I don't think there are very many. People didn't have the money for film or developing back then, not with the war on. But I'll see what I can find."

"Sadie, would you like coffee?" Debbie asked. "Or tea? Anything? We have hot chocolate too. If you'd prefer."

Sadie stood, scooping the doll back into its bag. "I've got to get back. The girls have their Tuesday violin lessons with Miss Rita." She clutched the bag tighter to her chest. "Thank you. I didn't know where to turn. I don't want the police involved yet, because if there's something unsavory in my family history, I want to know first."

"Call me if you find any photos," Janet said as Sadie moved to the door. "We'll come over and check them out with you."

"I will." She hurried out the door. The brewing storm slapped drops of slush around her as she dashed across the parking lot.

"You got your wish," Debbie noted as she stood. She crossed the room and flicked off the lights.

"The only thing I'm wishing is that I'd worn a coat today."

"I meant the other wish." Debbie moved toward the door. "The one about not liking quiet days. Sadie's visit took care of that, didn't it?"

Janet agreed. Sadie's request had put a whole new spin on the day. "It sure did. And just when I think I'm relegated to dashing to your car in this slop, a hero comes along." She smiled as Ian pulled up to the curb.

But as she and Debbie hurried to their cars, the brooch in her pocket claimed her thoughts. Whose was it? Why was it hidden in a musty doll then left, forgotten, in an old trunk?

And how did some anonymous person know about it?

That might be the biggest question of all.

CHAPTER TWO

Ian faced Sadie later that evening. He held the brooch in one hand and a small magnifying glass in the other. "Sadie, you told Janet and Debbie that you found this inside an old doll, correct?"

Though her friend had expressed reluctance to involve the police, Janet had promised that her husband would be discreet, while his involvement would provide a measure of protection in an uncertain situation. Sadie had eventually come around and agreed to come over and talk to Ian.

Sadie reached into her bag and brought out the rag doll. "Yes, although I'd never have thought of looking inside on my own." She fingered the body of the doll. "I worked it loose with a butter knife and found the little satin bag. I might never have known it was there if I hadn't been prodded by the email."

He let out a low whistle while Janet scoped out vintage brooches on the internet. Debbie had taken the seat across from Sadie at the kitchen table. She typed notes into her phone as they talked.

"I don't see any identifiers." Ian had put his reading glasses on to examine the brooch. He peered up, over them. "Initials or engravings. That kind of thing."

Sadie frowned. "I know. I checked it too, hoping for something. There's nothing."

He set down the brooch. "No one in the family ever mentioned this? Or misplacing it?"

"No. I'm assuming the last time someone saw the doll was in 1950, which is the date on the newspapers in the trunk. Of course, I could be totally wrong about that, and maybe it was put in years later or years before. There's no way of knowing." Sadie took a sip of tea. "Like I told you earlier, the trunk came with Gigi. I was about six when Great-Grandpa Joe died and she moved in with Aunt Lena. That would have been around 1986."

"Sadie, you mentioned your grandma Mary this morning," Janet said. "Was she older than Lena?"

"She was," Sadie told her. "By quite a bit, I think. Grandma Mary was born in Ireland, and Aunt Lena and Uncle Michael were born here in the States. When they were adults, Mary and Michael married and moved away from Dennison, but Lena stayed to help take care of Gigi and Grandpa Joe."

"So if Gigi—Annie—came to live with Lena in the mideighties, you must have seen the trunk in the attic at some point," Ian said.

"No one ever wanted to go into Aunt Lena's attic," Sadie explained. "She was a wonderful woman, and she and I were especially close, but her attic was way too spooky for kids' adventures. She didn't believe in throwing anything away, and if we kids ever did venture up there, the mice greeted us at the top of the stairs. She set traps now and then but didn't like to go up the stairs to retrieve them. You could hear the skitters when you stayed overnight. Drew and I cleared everything out after she passed and hired an exterminator to go on a major mouse removal expedition."

Debbie shuddered. "That sounds like a massive project."

Sadie chuckled. "I suppose it didn't help that my brother, John, and I made up scary stories about what happened to people up there. We had ourselves so spooked we wouldn't even walk past the door that led to the attic."

"How did your family end up in Dennison?" Janet asked.

"My great-grandparents and Grandma came over from Ireland after World War II, and they had very little," Sadie said. "Grandma was a girl at the time, of course. They came into New York Harbor and lived in Cleveland for a while. Then Great-Grandpa Joe got a job with the Pennsylvania Railroad. They assigned him to Dennison, and that's how we got here. He ran a route for a long time, long enough to get his twenty-five-year pin with them."

Janet exchanged looks with Debbie. "We can ask Eileen if she knew him," she said. "And Harry too." Eileen Palmer and Harry Franklin had both worked at the station around that time.

"They lived up the road from your house, Debbie," Sadie added. "Just beyond the curve that heads out of town."

"Then Ray might have known them too," Debbie said, referring to Ray Zink, her home's previous owner. "At least that gives us some leads to start with."

Janet picked up the brooch. "Sadie, were you able to find any pictures of your grandmother or great-grandparents?"

"Yes," Sadie said. "Several, in fact." She stood, retrieved a folder from the kitchen counter, and handed it over.

Janet opened the folder and shuffled through the black-and-white photos. Most of them were staged shots of a family through the years. Janet studied the one that looked most recent. From their clothes and hairstyles, she thought it must have been taken sometime in the fifties. She flipped it over and saw she was right. Someone had written *1953 Mary-19, Lena-7, Michael-5* on the back.

She studied the faces on the front of the photo. The oldest girl—Mary, according to the label—had a much fairer complexion than the rest of the family. "Now I see where Bria gets her lighter hair and skin color," she said to Sadie. "She takes after your grandma Mary."

"She does," Sadie replied. "The girls are twins, but they're nothing alike, in looks or temperament. Bria is more contemplative and serious, like Grandma Mary, and Brooke is more carefree, like Drew's side of the family. It's hard to get her to be serious about anything."

"She'll learn to be serious as she gets older. She should have fun as a child," Janet said with a smile.

Sadie traced a finger over the photo in Janet's hand. "I wish I knew more about my ancestors. When I was in college, I had a class project to trace my family tree, but my father put the hammer down on that real quick. He made it clear that my grandmother didn't talk about the war or coming over or any of that, and Dad said it wasn't because she didn't remember things. He said she didn't want to say or do anything that might get her parents into trouble, so she put it behind her and kept whatever secrets they had."

Her words triggered Janet's curiosity. "That's how he phrased it? Keeping whatever secrets they had?"

"Well, I told you I know my family has secrets," Sadie said.

"But secrets that could get them into trouble?" Debbie asked. "They were from Ireland. What secrets about the war could have gotten them in trouble in America?"

Sadie shrugged. "I have no idea, but those were the words he used. So I couldn't complete the project. And with both Gigi and

Aunt Lena gone now, there's no one left to ask about the doll. Or the brooch. I can't imagine Joe and Annie Harper doing anything wrong, but who's to say what kind of things people had to do in the face of poverty and aggression? Drew always wanted to ask Grandma about it, but he never did because I asked him not to. After she lived through the war and everything else, I couldn't bear the idea of causing her any more distress."

Debbie nodded. "And Lena was a lot younger than your grandmother, so—"

"She was born after the war ended, so she was way too young to remember anything." Sadie finished the thought for her. "Although now I wish I'd asked before she passed away. She was always respectful of Grandma's wishes as far as I know, but they were sisters. She might have known something, because sisters share secrets. And after Gigi and Great-Grandpa Joe passed, what harm would there have been to tell what she knew?"

"Sometimes sisters share secrets," Debbie said. "But not all the time."

Sadie's frown deepened. "I can't get that email out of my head. Someone knows the doll held a secret. How did they know that unless they had something to do with it? And what are the odds of that person seeing the rag doll on That's My Baby's social media page?"

"Either an unusual coincidence…" Debbie began.

"Or that person has a reason to watch your page," Janet added.

Sadie shivered.

"Not necessarily a bad reason," Janet said quickly. "It could be as simple as the person is a distant family member. Someone from the

Harper family, or someone who knew Aunt Lena years ago. She started the doll hospital in the eighties as a cottage industry, right?"

"That's right. She started it shortly before Gigi came to live with her."

"So it's quite possible that this person follows the page because they knew Lena or worked with her or something," Janet said. "Although your post obviously triggered something from the past for them. I would guess that's not unusual for people who've gone through a war."

"You think it's nefarious?" Sadie picked up the brooch.

"I hope not, but it *is* a mystery, and it bears looking into," Janet said firmly. "I don't like that they used an anonymous email, but a lot of people guard their privacy. Like your grandmother did. And there's still the question of how they knew something was inside the doll. Unless it was a family thing at some point. Or something Lena mentioned a long time ago. We know she was just this side of a hoarder. Maybe she had a habit of putting things in safe places and then forgetting where they were."

"I do that all the time," Sadie admitted.

"Me too," Debbie said. "Did you try sending a return email like we talked about, Sadie?"

Sadie grimaced. "As soon as I got home from running the girls to their lesson, but it bounced right back with an automated response that the address didn't accept emails. So maybe whoever this is will see it or maybe not. We won't know unless they write back, I guess."

"I'd like to see people guard their privacy more than they do now," Ian said. "But not much is kept under wraps anymore."

"Except this, apparently." Sadie set the brooch on the table and stood, clutching the doll. "I've got to get home. Drew's on overnight at the hospital, and even though the girls are old enough to be on their own, morning comes early. That's my time to catch up on laundry and housework, since the evenings are too full to get much done. Are you sure you don't mind keeping the brooch?"

Ian slipped the brooch into its pouch. "Not at all. And Sadie, I don't think the person who reached out to you did so with malice, but the truth is we don't know why he or she wants anonymity. Let me know if they have further contact with you, all right?"

"I will," she promised. "The anonymous thing threw me for a loop too. It seems unnecessary, but maybe it's like you said." She shifted her attention to Debbie and Janet. "Maybe they like their privacy."

"We'll let you know what we find out," Janet promised as she stood and walked Sadie to the door.

"Thank you," Sadie said. "Talking it out has made me feel better."

"Good." Janet offered her a reassuring smile, but once Sadie was in her car, Janet shut the door and returned to Ian and Debbie in the kitchen. "Did the words 'trouble' and 'secrets' leap out at you guys?"

"Considering the possible World War II time frame, I don't find that a big stretch," Ian said. "There was plenty of trouble everywhere, and most people had secrets."

"But we're talking about Ireland." Debbie made the point as she typed something into her phone. "Not your classic Allies vs. Axis war fronts."

Janet raised an eyebrow. "What do you mean?"

"I took a class on World War II my sophomore year of college," she explained. "It covered the countries that declared war and those that declared neutrality, like Ireland. They were so committed to not taking a side that when thousands of Irish soldiers joined the British forces, they were listed as deserters, as if they were traitors to Ireland. The country finally pardoned them about ten years ago. How crazy is that? They needed a pardon for fighting the atrocities of Hitler because their country declared neutrality."

"You can't be serious." Janet couldn't believe such a thing.

"It's true. A lot of smaller countries declared neutrality. They believed if they got involved, they would be wiped off the face of the earth." She splayed her hands. "And when you look at it that way, it becomes more understandable why they didn't get involved."

"Whether they got involved or not, countries like that had to be in the thick of things even if they didn't want to be," Ian said. "I'm pretty sure you didn't have to be in the war to be surrounded by loss and rationing and a rising black market."

"Of course." Janet sat down across from Debbie. "The black market. If that's the time frame we're talking about." Although the doll might have been in the style of the World War II era, it could have been made before or after the actual war. Pinpointing the doll's age could be crucial to their investigation. "Black markets rose up all over the place when supplies got scarce. We can add that to our list of possibilities. People can get creative when they want to smuggle something."

Debbie made a note in her phone and rose from the table. "Maybe we can set up a meeting with Eileen and Ray after work tomorrow." She tugged on her winter coat. "I sure won't mind when it's mild enough to hang this baby up for the summer."

"I'm with you on that." Janet walked her to the door while Ian stashed the brooch in the safe they'd installed behind a small bookcase. "Starting tomorrow, I'm hanging a sweatshirt at the café for the next time I foolishly anticipate an early spring."

"Did you make a note about the shamrock cakes and cookies?" Debbie asked as she went out the door.

"I put a reminder on my phone, and a fresh supply of green food coloring came in today," Janet replied. "I'll have Celtic-themed treats in the case tomorrow, and I'm adding mint to some of them for the full effect."

"Patricia will be thrilled."

Janet laughed. Patricia Franklin was Harry Franklin's granddaughter, and she was known for her attorney skills as well as her love of peppermint flavoring in her hot chocolates, coffees, and mochas. Harry, almost ninety-six years old, had been a porter for the railroad during World War II and then a conductor after. Long since retired, Harry lived nearby, and he and his dog, Crosby, frequented the café on a daily basis. Harry was a born storyteller, and his memory was sharp. Patricia made it a point to stop by the café almost every morning, ostensibly for a delicious coffee but probably to check on her grandfather without making it obvious. "She'll be in her happy place for certain. See you in the morning."

Debbie didn't bother zipping her jacket but hugged it around her middle as she dashed to her car. Janet waited until Debbie got to her car and started the engine, and then she pushed the door shut and locked it.

She had to wake up early to get the café ovens fired up, but before she went to bed, she crossed the floor to check one more thing on her laptop. She put some keywords into the search bar, and a flood of information streamed onto the screen—links to articles about people hiding things away to keep them out of the hands of the Nazis and the Russians as their armies seized city after city in their quest for domination.

Could Sadie's family have used rag dolls to transport precious items when they fled their homeland, perhaps packed as war raged on all around them? Could there be more dolls like this one hidden in Lena's belongings?

Ian let Laddie out for one last time that evening. When the dog trotted back inside and performed his customary three-circle spin before settling down on the rug, Janet closed the laptop.

They'd left the café a few hours before with little to go on. An hour of talking and internet browsing had opened doors to multiple possibilities that could give them a starting point.

It wasn't much, but it was better than what they had before.

Kielce, Poland
August 30, 1939

Sweet Nessie!

How good to get your letter acknowledging the receipt of my gift to you, dear sister. It will suit your new home as you've described it to me, and though I know it's not newly built, it is new to you and therefore quite a blessing. The warmth of old homes isn't in the tones of paint or even the setting amongst neighbors. It is in the heart of the family who lives therein, and your sweet family will bring abundant blessings to those walls. Two children, growing well. Who could ask for more than my dearest sister has been granted?

I am practicing my English as you suggested. I do it often when I am alone. Joseph does not have as much opportunity, but when he is home, he practices with me. It is good to know another language, and I am so glad our mother insisted on that from our birth. Oh, how I argued with her, remember? To leave the farm and go off to an English school seemed like punishment back then, and how I protested. I'm ashamed to say so now.

But you, ever obedient, learned and then guided me. I am glad that your knowledge breaks down walls for you there in your new country.

And let me add here that working on the last project I sent to you was a constant source of goodness and light. A true work of my hands, putting my heart in motion. It took longer than any other project I've put forth, but it was well worth the expense and exertion. Even Joseph says so, and you know my Joseph is a man of few words. He puts God and effort first, knowing it takes both to build a family no matter where one lives, although the sadness of separation is a bitter pill for both of us. I know you understand that.

All is well here.

Our cousins regularly check on the wheat crop, and Uncle Ludwig monitors the moisture content in hopes of a harvest soon. The wheat field lies to the east this year. We rotate it from area to area, sweetening the soil with leavings from the seven cows I milk twice daily. We would love to get the ripe grains into a silo soon. Rain comes as it will, and we need the grain to be dry enough to store. Accomplishing the harvest between downpours is always a trick, although this summer has been dry. Even though the wheat isn't so tall, the harvest looks to be plentiful.

My sewing continues as it can, but a necessary pause to harvest and preserve early vegetables and fruits has left my treadle quiet these last few days. I will catch up soon, I am certain. Busy hands, you know! I am praying all is well there, for each of you. Lack of news is a concern, and I miss hearing from you, but I pray for you and yours daily. You are on my mind. Share my love with everyone.

It is two days later, Nessie. Two days...and such differences here.

So much has happened.

So much has turned upside down that I do not know where to begin to describe it, but surely it made the news even that far away, how Germany has swept in and taken over. It is hard to know what to say and what to do. With Joseph working, the rest of us plod on, eyes on what must be done, for that is all we know. Conscription to service has begun, and it is as if dark clouds loom despite the sunniest of days. Pray for us, Nessie. For all of us here in this land, for we know not what is to come, and although I refuse to live in fear, I know well to embrace a layer of caution.

God be with you, my sweet sister. Pray for us. For all of us. Please.

Your sister,

Anya

CHAPTER THREE

Good Shepherd Retirement Center is closed?" Janet frowned, sure she hadn't heard the depot museum curator correctly.

"*Temporarily* closed to visitors," Kim Smith explained as she organized papers on her ticket-window desk. Kim ran the depot museum, but during slower days in winter she also operated the ticket counter and the phones. "They're trying to contain a late-season flu outbreak, so they put the no-visitors mandate in place for the next seven days. They'll reassess the situation then. As you can imagine, my mother is champing at the bit."

Janet had known Eileen Palmer for years. Kim's mother had run the busy depot during World War II. She had married and raised her family in Dennison. Eileen had been a regular customer at the Third Street Bakery, where Janet had worked until the bakery owners retired—around the same time Debbie called her with the idea of opening a café in the depot.

"I bet she is," Janet replied. "Your mother isn't a sit-back-and-wait kind of person, despite her age."

"I almost think it's more *because* of her age," said Kim. "She says she's well beyond the stage of planting young trees or buying green bananas, so let's live life while we've got it. But the facilities medical director decided a seven-day lockdown was best for the residents, and we all want to keep them safe. I told her she could stay with us for the week, but she said she felt it was her duty to stay there and help her friends pass the time."

"Selfless as always," Janet said fondly. "I'm sure her friends will appreciate her 'all for one and one for all' attitude."

Kim acknowledged Janet with a wry grin. "In any case, she's going to make the most of the moratorium. She's not up to starting a crochet project right now, but she said there's a new supply of those three-dimensional art kits in stock, and she's going to keep herself busy doing some of those. Between naps. Her words. Not mine."

"Then we'll put off seeing her and Ray until they open things back up," Janet said. She briefly considered calling Eileen instead but dismissed that notion right away. For a centenarian, Eileen's hearing was good, but it wasn't that good.

An alarm sounded on Janet's phone. "Oops, the chocolate-mint cupcakes are calling me. Gotta go." She hurried into the café and past Debbie, who was washing her hands after prepping the register.

In the kitchen, Janet pulled three trays of cupcakes from the ovens, settled them onto the tiered cooling rack, and breathed in the delicious aroma. The fourth tray she carried into the dining area and placed on the counter. "This has got to be one of the best combo smells in the world," she said to no one in particular.

"Right up there with coffee and chocolate," Harry offered. He'd come in for his daily breakfast. Sometimes he ordered a hot meal, but today he was opting for coffee and a cinnamon roll. Crosby was curled up at his feet.

"I vote hazelnut and chocolate," said Debbie as she topped up Harry's coffee.

"The common denominator is always chocolate. You won't get an argument from me on that," Janet said. "Chocolate-based any-thing is good. On another note, we won't be visiting Eileen for a while, because there's a flu lockdown at Good Shepherd."

"Oh dear," Debbie said. "Flu can be rough on the elderly, so it's probably a wise idea on their part. But we've got Harry right here." She arched her left brow.

Janet took the hint. "Harry, do you remember working with a man named Joe Harper sometime after the war ended?"

"Joe?" He beamed, clearly excited to share the memory with them. "I sure do. That man understood more about making a train run smoothly than ten men put together, and that's no exaggeration. Joe Harper had a knack for fixing a problem before other guys even sensed it coming. He used to say he could hear things in the engine that called to him. He was a solid asset to this depot. He ran passenger trains until they stopped coming through over fifty years back. Then he ran freight trains for another dozen years before retiring. He was a good man and a hard worker. Always had his head on straight." That was high praise coming from Harry.

"He had family here, right?" Debbie asked.

"He did, sure enough," Harry said. "A wife and a few kids. I remember his oldest girl, Mary. Such a pale, quiet little thing. There was quite an age gap between her and the younger two. A full decade and a little more."

"Did Vernon know any of the Harper kids?" Janet asked. Vernon was Harry's son and Patricia's dad.

"He did. He went to school with Michael, the youngest, and he knew Lena. Like I said, Mary was much older. He didn't meet her until after he and Ruth were married."

"How did they meet?" Debbie asked.

Harry took another bite of his cinnamon roll and washed it down with a gulp of coffee. "In the early seventies, Vernon and Ruth were at the courthouse in New Philly applying for a permit to get some work done on their house when Mary came in searching for a record of her birth. They never found it, though. Evidently, it burned to a crisp in a fire back in Ireland. At least I think that's what Ruth told me. If that was the case, there wouldn't have been anything anyone could have done to help. Proving who you were wasn't as easy as it is now. The only reason I remember is because Ruth and Vernon found Mary crying in the hallway. They comforted her, and Ruth really felt for her."

"Do you think Ruth would remember Mary?" Janet asked.

Harry nodded. "I expect she'd remember Mary because that scene at the courthouse touched her heart. Vernon and Ruth have a pair of good hearts, that's certain. I'm sure they'd be happy to answer some questions, and Ruth loves company."

He reached for his mug as Patricia came through the door. He turned her way, and his face lit up, his joyful expression warming Janet's heart.

"Good morning, all!" Patricia sang out. She gave her grandpa a kiss on the cheek and settled on the stool next to him, smiling at Janet. "I'd love one of those," she said, pointing to the half-eaten roll on Harry's plate.

"What can we get you to drink? Your usual?" Debbie suggested.

Patricia shivered and shrugged out of her coat. "That sounds wonderful. Would you make it extra hot? And I'll take the largest size you offer. That cold, damp wind cuts through me like a knife. I saw a couple of those glossy green shamrocks dancing across the parking lot, on their way to who knows where." Kim and a couple of volunteers had decorated the outside of the depot with St. Patrick's Day bits and pieces they'd found at a dollar store. Patricia lifted a hand to her carefully styled hair. "I'd have chased after them, but a wind like that works to undo what took me thirty minutes to get done, and no one has time for that with a video meeting as the first thing on the schedule for the day. Maybe it's me, but it feels as if the winds that tunnel down the tracks and across the creek are fiercer than ever these days."

"It's been crazy windy lately," Debbie agreed as she plated Patricia's gooey cinnamon roll.

"Do I smell chocolate-mint cupcakes, Janet?" Patricia hiked both brows in anticipation.

"You do. That's impressive," Janet said. "I still have to pipe the frosting."

"Well, I'm going to need four of those later today," Patricia declared. "My mama put me on to mixing chocolate and peppermint when I was real small, and a box of those cupcakes will bring a smile to her face. It would be a nice treat for her and Dad, although he's supposed to be watching his sweets. But then, longevity seems to run in the family." She smiled at Harry. "So I don't fret too much."

The creases edging Harry's eyes deepened when he returned her smile. "The Lord's been good to me, no denying that. Long life, good health, loving family. I've got no complaints. At the moment," he added with a wink. "Me and Crosby—we're doing all right."

Janet finished layering Patricia's mocha and handed it over. "Would you mind if we deliver the cupcakes to your parents? We're hoping to ask your mother about a woman she met in the seventies. Harry said they had a moment that stuck with her for a long time."

"I'd love for you to do that," Patricia said. "They recently got back from their annual trip to see Mom's side of the family, and I'm sure she'd be delighted to see you. It'll also save me a trip back here at lunch. Go ahead and add the price of the cupcakes to my bill. But call them before you swing by, all right? Just to make sure they're not gallivanting somewhere and will be at home."

"We will," promised Janet. The café's phone rang, and by the time she'd written down the to-go order, Patricia was gone. Janet went into the kitchen and called Patricia's parents. Ruth sounded happy that they were stopping by, and Janet was too. Vernon and Ruth were wonderful to be around, so the visit would be pleasant whether they were able to give her new information or not.

That being said, she couldn't deny that she deeply hoped they could answer some of her questions. And she had many.

Kielce, Poland
December 1939

Christmas greetings, my loves! I don't know if this will reach you in a timely fashion, yet I send our love to you and yours. I do not know what you have heard of our situation here. My beloved Joseph works on, so dependable and good! He is appreciated by those in authority and has the commendations to show it. The railroad knows his value in these trying times. They keep him running some of the more difficult routes as he has always done. Good travel and access are vital in so many ways.

We all put our hands and backs to the harvest. Neighbors came to help. The thrasher was not useful with trodden wheat, so we gleaned like Ruth of the Bible. We carried baskets and gathered until evening, day after day. What some might call meager, we call a blessing.

The weather has turned fully now. Cold has descended. The darkening clouds and short days steal the light, but that gives us more time for rest, which we need every bit as much as productivity.

I sew by day. My skills have been noticed by some of the new ladies in town, and I have been commissioned to make lovely gowns. Thus, I am now able to put Mama's and Baba's dressmaking lessons to work after my skills went unused through so many years of want. The chance to practice my sewing keeps my mind sharp through the long days of winter. The work brings thoughts of you and me, sitting at Baba's feet, watching her needle fly as fast as her tongue. She taught us much and taught us well. Her strength and her faith are with me each day now, a gift that went unappreciated when I was a child, but that builds my strength and determination now. Her words of wisdom carry me through.

The light wanes. I must close. As ever...

Your beloved sister,

Anya

CHAPTER FOUR

When Janet and Debbie arrived at the Franklins' New Philadelphia home that afternoon, Vernon met them at the door. "Come on in, ladies," he said. "Let's get you out of that wind."

They hurried in, and Vernon shut the door behind them. "I don't know why nature sees fit to make winter last weeks beyond what I want it to, but it's been that way as long as I can remember, and that's quite a while," he said. "Ruth's through here." He led them to the kitchen. "And we're both very happy to have company."

"And chocolate-mint cupcakes!" Ruth called. The kitchen was nicely updated with quartz countertops and white cabinetry with gold hardware. "What a pleasure, ladies. Come on in, have a seat. Coffee or tea for either of you?"

"Yes please," Debbie said. "Coffee for me."

"And I'll have a cup of tea." Janet set the bakery box of cupcakes on the kitchen table and opened it. "We come bearing gifts, as promised."

"With an ulterior motive," Debbie added. "Though not a bad one. Harry said you might remember something from a few years ago that could help us solve a puzzle we're working on."

"Harry has mentioned more than once how the pair of you are good at figuring things out." Ruth set their mugs on the table. "And he likes that you pick his brain now and again. He says it helps him stay sharp." She took a seat next to Vernon and across from Janet and Debbie. "What can we help you with?"

"Can you tell us anything about Mary Harper?" Janet asked, getting right to the point.

Ruth's expression became thoughtful. "Well, the Harpers were good folks, not that I knew them well. Harry worked with Joe, and they got on fine. I didn't know Mrs. Harper at all. I never saw her. I heard she stayed home, sewing up a storm, so our paths never crossed. But still, I never heard of them causing any kind of trouble. They kept largely to themselves, but some people are shy, and there's nothing wrong with that."

Debbie began tapping notes into her phone.

Ruth went on. "But you're asking about Mary, and that's a different story. She was a striking woman, with skin so pale and hair so blond it was almost white. I imagine Dad told you about the day we saw her at the county clerk's office. We had gone by to pick up a permit for some changes we were doing on our first place, and we were so excited." She smiled at Vernon. "Remember, honey?"

"I do," he said. "Adding that deck was one of the best ideas you've ever had."

"We used it enough to get our money's worth, that's for sure." Ruth took a sip of her tea. "Anyway, that's when we met Mary."

"Harry said she was looking for her birth records." Janet blew on her coffee.

Ruth leaned closer. "Mary Harper was trying to find her birth records, one way or another. I don't know why. Maybe she was wondering if she'd been adopted or something. She said she'd written to the church in Ireland only to find that it had suffered a fire fifteen years before and all the records were lost. And of course, back then, the records were kept on paper, so if it was gone, it was gone. They told her they didn't have any backup recordkeeping, and that was that."

"How sad," Debbie murmured.

"It was like that sometimes back then, folks not having proof of identity. It sounds crazy to us now, but that's how it was for so many. The laws about it weren't changed until after the war. That meant Mary's little brother and sister were both registered, but there was nothing on her."

"That must have been so frustrating for her," Janet observed.

"It was," Ruth confirmed. "I had never met her, but I knew who she was. I couldn't simply stand there and not try to help her. We sat on the bench outside the clerk's window, and I tried to comfort her while she cried."

Debbie put her hand over Ruth's. "That was a really kind thing to do."

Ruth smiled. "Vernon and I were there for such a happy reason. We'd just closed on our first home—it was so tiny, but how we loved it!—and I simply couldn't abide the sadness in her eyes. My life's been so good in most every way that matters. I hope she finally found what she was after."

"Did Mary say anything to you?" Debbie asked. "Share what was wrong?"

"She wanted to know her story." Compassion softened Ruth's expression. "She said that what she remembered felt right and wrong at the same time. I remember her words like it was yesterday. She said, 'I guess I'll never know the truth.'"

"'The truth'?"

Ruth didn't seem to notice the heightened interest in Janet's tone. "About where she was born," she explained, but Janet wondered if there was more to it than that.

Ruth shrugged. "That was the extent of it. I gave her my hankie, and she went off to live her life. I did the same. I'd see her now and again around town. She always had a sweet smile and a kind word for me, but I always suspected that a lot of Marys were out there. People who wouldn't be able to verify where they came from, something most of us take for granted."

Debbie gulped the last of her tea. "We sure appreciate this, Ruth. You've been a big help."

Ruth patted her hand. "Happy to help any way I can."

"And I hope you love these cupcakes," Janet added as she stood. Debbie followed suit. "It's my grandmother's dark-chocolate cake recipe, which I guarded with my life until I realized that it's actually the recipe on the back of the cocoa container."

Ruth burst out laughing. "My mama made a delicious lemon cake. She carted it to so many church suppers and neighborhood gatherings that people named it after her. Then about five years ago, Patricia discovered that Mama's so-called 'secret' recipe had been featured in dozens of ladies' magazines in the fifties. But we still call it 'Marybelle's Luscious Lemon Cake,' even knowing she nipped it out of a magazine way back when."

"Thank you, Ruth." Janet reached out a hand to the older woman. "We're grateful for your time and your recollection."

Her smile deepened. "Come back anytime, ladies." She stood and pulled Janet in for a hug. "It did me good to have a nice sit-down conversation with the two of you. It's an absolute pleasure to have company come by."

"For us too," Debbie assured her as they hugged.

Vernon saw them out, and when they got to the car, Janet exchanged a look with Debbie. "Mary was searching for the truth."

Debbie nodded. "And Sadie's father didn't want Sadie to ask Mary any questions about her past because Mary had decided to keep her parents' secrets so they wouldn't get into trouble. Does that mean that she eventually found out the truth?"

Janet gripped the wheel tightly as she started the engine. "What could Mary's parents have been into?"

"When it comes to the war and post-war, the list is long and the options are many," Debbie replied as Janet backed onto the road. "But I think it's a safe bet that something was going on."

Janet couldn't disagree. "We've got no proof yet, but it does seem as if the Harpers came across the Atlantic with their share of secrets. Now we need to figure out if one of the secrets involved that brooch."

"And why a random stranger sent such a strange message over a doll," Debbie said.

"I've got my grandmother's brooch," Janet mused as they headed down the road. "Not as old as that one, but lovely. I'd be devastated if it disappeared one day, but wartime is different." She eased through a yield sign. "Lots of stuff went missing during the war. People are still hunting things down eighty years later. We hear stories all the time about precious artifacts being found and returned to their rightful place after being hidden or stolen by one faction or another. Maybe it's not so strange that there's a brooch in the doll. Maybe it was simple precaution."

"If that's the case, wouldn't that person have retrieved it at some point?" Debbie asked. "Or wouldn't someone else have stumbled on it eventually? It's a valuable brooch, an heirloom-style piece, so why wouldn't someone at least know about it? Talk about it? Lament its loss? Wouldn't that have been more normal?"

"Misplaced? Forgotten?" Janet suggested as they approached Debbie's house.

"Maybe." Debbie didn't hide the skepticism in her voice or expression. "But the brooch is one part of our mystery. We still have the person who sent Sadie that email. Whoever it is knew there was something in the doll. Is this person a relative? Are they going to claim the brooch?"

Janet tapped the wheel. "Let's think on it more later. Since we can't visit with Eileen or Ray at Good Shepherd for a week, maybe we can try to find some information about the Harpers online. Mom has a membership on one of the big ancestry sites. Maybe we can trace Sadie's family back to Ireland. If we can track their roots to the town where the church burned, that could help." She flipped on her turn signal. "We can also ask Sadie. She might know what part of Ireland her family comes from."

"It wouldn't hurt," Debbie agreed. "I'd like to poke around Lena's attic too. If the doll lay undiscovered for decades, there might be other clues hidden up there."

"And mice," Janet noted, wrinkling her nose. "But if the exterminator did a decent job, they shouldn't be as bad as they used to be. I can handle the odd mouse well enough, but I'm not a fan of legions of rogue rodents lurking in the shadows."

"Me either."

Janet pulled into Debbie's driveway then twisted in her seat to face her friend. "I'll see you in the morning. I promised my mom I'd make more cinnamon rolls this week, and there's time tomorrow. She gave up chocolate for Lent. She's done well so far, but she's hankering for something non-chocolate and delicious. Cinnamon rolls fit the bill, and Harry will love them too."

"Greg loves them as well," Debbie said as she stepped onto the asphalt driveway. "And the boys, although they declared a firm tie between your cinnamon rolls and the giant chocolate chip cookies."

Janet laughed. "Smart kids. Like their dad," she teased, and this time Debbie didn't pretend that Greg Connor was merely another customer.

She leaned in, winked, and smiled. "Smart," she agreed. "And real cute. But that's a discussion for another day." She shut the door and waved as she hurried toward her porch. "See you tomorrow!"

Janet waved back. She thought about Ruth's words as she made the short trek to her own house. Sadie's grandmother had been searching for some kind of truth in her past. Sadie wanted the very same thing.

If Janet and Debbie found the right path to take, maybe they would figure out a way to answer both women's questions.

Kielce, Poland
February 1940

Oh, my dearest Nessie, it was so nice to hear from you! I am overjoyed that all goes well there in your new home. How wonderful to hear that the children play, work, and grow as all children should, dear sister!

Your adventures in a new land sound so daring to a homebody like me, but I do love reading about your time there. And the thought of your extra room inspired me to share my gifts once more. After all, your new home should feel as much like a home as possible, should it not? A new package will arrive soon. I know you will love it, dearest Nessie!

I have also sent along a toy similar to what you and I played with as children in Baba's home, those old rag dolls we loved so well! Baba wasted nothing, did she? Even making us dolls with bits of this and that. Frugal and clever, Baba taught us well, especially when Mama was busy with the farm or the men's needs for food and clothing. I am making more clothing these days. So many lovely things, Nessie. It is an unexpected opportunity for me, and one I don't take lightly.

Although the light has been short, I have been blessed to work with some lovely materials for the ladies who have come to town. They let me keep the remnants, a wonderful thing for someone like me who sees scraps as puzzle pieces. Clever piecing allows the bits to become part of a whole once more. It is a good pastime for one whose options have changed of late.

Our cousins have been taken into service, so it is just the two of us here. Three when Marysia visits. But often I am a group of one, as odd as that feels in our big, sprawling family.

My newest gift to you should arrive in a few weeks' time. How many weeks? How is one to know? But Joseph will check on that for me and send word.

Blessings to you as spring approaches. It will be met with great affection here, as I'm sure it will be there.

Lent begins...and I offer my sacrifices to Him who sacrificed all for me.

Your beloved sister,

Anya

CHAPTER FIVE

Janet tied the bandanna firmly around her hair as they approached the doll hospital's attic door two days later.

"Irrational fear of cobwebs?" Debbie teased as Sadie reached for the doorknob.

"Nope," Janet replied. "I can wash out cobwebs, but ever since I read that passage in the Little House books about a mouse cutting Charles's hair in his sleep to line its nest, I don't take any chances." She stretched out her gloved hands for proof. "Just in case."

"I didn't know we planned on sleeping up there," Sadie said. She and Debbie exchanged a grin. "I would have brought my jammies along."

"Nowhere is it written that mice only claim hair from sleeping victims," Janet shot back. "And I don't need one dropping from the trusses onto my bare head."

"Well, I haven't heard, seen, or smelled any mice in weeks, so I think we're okay, but you know how it goes." Sadie led the way upstairs. "If you see one mouse, you've got seven. So there's that."

Janet groaned, but nothing scurried out of their way as they got to the top of the stairs. The attic opened wide in front of them.

"If this was as full as you said, then you've really done a number up here, Sadie," Debbie said. "There's almost nothing left. Nice work."

Sadie acknowledged her comment as she tugged on her own pair of gloves. "We donated and tossed so much, and by the time we were done with that, the whole house felt lighter. Aunt Lena wasn't alive during the Great Depression, but she still felt the need to stash things in every available nook and cranny." She scanned the shadowed attic as she moved forward with a pair of emergency lanterns to offer more light. "If something could possibly be used in the next twenty years, she stored it and then forgot its existence. Or couldn't find it. When I reorganized the supply shelves in the doll-repair room, I was amazed at the amount of useless stuff tucked away. Not old doll pieces, mind you. Those could be helpful. But so many unrelated things that had no reason to be there."

"Or no reason apparent to our generation," Janet pointed out.

Sadie acknowledged that with a nod. "True enough. On a positive note, that doesn't leave us with much to go through," she said as they began to explore the attic's now meager contents. "I did get rid of the old dress forms that John used to scare us with."

Janet chuckled, remembering John's mischievous nature. "He'd dress them up and have them waiting in your closet to scare us. I'm sure they heard us shrieking in the next county."

"He was incredibly resourceful...and an unmitigated brat," Sadie said.

Janet laughed as she slid open a drawer on a small dresser. She pulled the knob carefully and ignored Debbie's snicker behind her.

No mice.

The drawer was empty altogether.

Thank heavens. She released the breath she was holding. "Now he's the sweetest guy. Fixes cars at reasonable prices and helps on two church committees. And he's still funny."

"He's definitely improved." Sadie pointed to the drawer Janet had opened. "That held old lace hankies and neck ribbons that had seen better days. They'd been chewed up and used for multiple nests, I'm sure. I tossed all of them then scrubbed away the mouse evidence because it's such a cute piece." She aimed a fond smile at the dresser. "I have no spot for it at my place, but I didn't want to donate it or scrap it. Both my girls declined when I offered to paint it for their rooms."

"It is super cute." Janet followed the curve of the small dresser with one hand. "You don't find this style in modern furniture. It's either pieced, or flat with a beveled edge. This takes artistry."

"What about Tiffany?" Debbie suggested from the opposite side of the dormered window. "She might like it, since she's getting an apartment next semester."

"I don't want to assume—" Janet began, but Sadie interrupted her.

"I'll text Drew and make sure it's okay with him, but if you think she'd like it, it's hers," Sadie said as she pulled her phone from her pocket. "I'm good with gaining any sense of order I can over here. It's different at my house. I'm used to my own clutter. I know what to keep and what to toss, but it's a whole other world when it's two-and-a-half floors of someone else's stuff piled here, there, and every-where. We're going to update Lena's apartment on the second floor and rent it out. The income should bring the doll repair hospital into the black at last."

"And that's a brilliant use of some really nice space." Janet smiled her approval as they hunted through the corners and around the few things left in the attic but found nothing of note.

After a few moments Sadie tugged a small trunk to the center. "This is where I found the doll. It had a few old figurines, some water glasses, and ten or twelve books. I gave all that to the Salvation Army."

Janet peered inside. "All that's left are a few scraps of material, a bobbin case, some seam tape, and a musty smell."

"Sadie, what do you know about the trunk itself?" Debbie snapped pictures of the interior then closed it to take a few more of the exterior.

"It's a piece of family history," Sadie said. "Down in the shop, I have one exactly like it but a little smaller that belonged to Annie."

"Did Joe and Annie bring the trunks over from Ireland?" Debbie asked.

"No. My great-great-aunt Nessie brought this one with her when she moved here in 1938. She was Annie's older sister and Grandma Mary's aunt. She and her husband, George, lived in New York. I've never met any of their descendants. Grandma Mary inherited this trunk when Nessie died."

Debbie raised the trunk's lid once more. "I want to get a better picture of this fabric." She lifted a dinner-platter-sized scrap and examined it.

"That's good-quality wool." Sadie took the piece from Debbie and rubbed it between her fingers. "The kind they used for dresses and suits. Not too heavy, and a fine thread that makes it stronger. Pricey goods."

"Ireland is famous for its wool," Janet remarked. "The Emerald Isle offers its sheep plenty of green grass, and fine wovens seem to come naturally. I wonder if anyone in the family worked in the woolens industry?" She touched the fabric in Debbie's hand. "Woolens were a major industry near the cities. I know this because my mom's been researching our family tree. and her great-grandmother worked in a uniform factory during both world wars. They used a lot of wool."

"I love history," Sadie said. "I wasn't happy when Dad thwarted my quest for information, but then I realized my love for my ancestors was stronger than my desire to learn their history." She dropped the piece of wool back into the trunk. "I might not have the past, but they gave me a future right here in this house."

"And a wonderful future it is." Janet hugged her arm. "Who's ready for a break? I brought some white-chocolate-frosted shamrock cakes along."

"I'm always ready for your baking," Sadie declared with a laugh.

The bell above the doll shop door jingled as they descended the stairs.

Janet and Debbie started toward the shop's small office as Sadie went forward to greet the customer. They hadn't gone far when they heard an angry male voice. They hurried to the front of store.

A man who seemed to be in his sixties stood inside the door. He was of average height and weight, and his hair was thinning on top.

He clutched a black-and-white picture in his right hand. It had faded, and the edges curled, but the images of a couple were clear. Sadie's eyes went wide when he brandished it, took two steps forward, and yelled, "Traitor!"

Sadie's mouth dropped open. She stared at him then at the photograph, then him again. "Who are you? And what are you talking about?"

The man's glare deepened. He waved the photograph as if to punctuate his point. "Your great-grandparents. The ones who turned their backs on everyone and everything they should have held dear. Traitors, both of them!"

"Now hold on," Sadie began, but the man continued his tirade.

"They denied who they were and what they'd done from the time they stepped off the boat. They hit American soil and kicked the Janek name off the dust of their German boots." He thumped his chest. "I'm a Janek. I'm not ashamed of it."

"*German* boots?" Sadie gaped at him.

He took a step forward then shook the picture again. His anger filled the small room with an almost tangible presence. Janet and Debbie drew close to Sadie's side in a firm show of support.

"Not one of you deserves what you've found in this country," he continued. "Not them." He shook the vintage photo to make his point. "Not their children or their children's children. I'm ashamed to know of you and more ashamed to be related to you!" He pivoted and stormed out the door.

He tried to slam it behind him, but the soft-closing mechanism Drew had installed made that impossible. That seemed to make the man angrier as he barreled past the large picture window facing the road.

He stomped to his car, yanked the driver's door open, and flung the photo onto the passenger seat before he climbed in. He started the engine then peeled out of the small parking area and onto the road, but not before Janet got a picture of his license plate.

Sadie stared after him, dumbfounded.

Debbie laid a hand on their friend's shoulder. "Sadie, who was he?"

Sadie shook her head, and her confused expression deepened. "I have no idea. I've never seen that man before in my life."

"Seriously?" Janet moved to flank Sadie's other side. "But he said he's related to you."

Sadie frowned. "I know. I heard that. But other than Gigi's sister, Nessie, and her family in New York City, I don't think we have relatives here. At least none I've ever met," she amended. "I don't know anything about Nessie's descendants, or even if she had any. If he is a relative, he's not a close one, because we did that family tree project in ninth grade. Remember? Dad helped me, and we went as far back as Gigi and Great-Grandpa Joe. They only had the two daughters, Lena and Grandma Mary."

Janet grinned. "I do remember. My mother gave me so much help that when Mrs. Heinz graded the reports, she told me I got an A and to tell my mother she got an A too. Mom was both embarrassed and delighted."

That made Debbie laugh. "I can totally see that." She sobered. "Sadie, are you sure about your relatives?"

"Positive. When we did that project, I drew out our family tree from Gigi and Great-Grandpa Joe right down to me and John. There were no lateral branches, no other Harpers. Just my great-great-aunt Nessie on the East Coast."

"And you said Nessie was Annie's older sister, right?" Janet took her phone from her pocket and made a few notes to jog her memory later.

Sadie glanced behind them, toward the gravel driveway they'd widened years back to allow several cars to park off the road. She twisted her hair around her finger, a nervous habit she'd had since elementary school. The man's surprise visit and tirade had undeniably bothered her. "Yes," she said. "We had no contact information for Nessie. I don't know why. It's sad that Gigi lost touch with her sister. But back then we couldn't exactly hop on the internet and find things with a few clicks."

"True." Janet held up her phone. "I texted Ian and asked him to come. And I got a picture of the guy's license plate. It's blurry, but clear enough to make out the number."

"We need to find out who he is," Sadie muttered. She raised a shaking hand to brush a lock of hair behind her ear. "Although, that name…Janek."

"What about it?" Janet asked eagerly.

Sadie faced Janet and Debbie. "I've heard that name before. About ten years ago. I remember hearing Grandma Mary say it to someone, maybe my mom. She said something about having some Janeks in the family, way back. I'm sure I wouldn't remember it otherwise, but I asked her about it later, and she told me to forget she ever said it. I haven't heard the name again until today."

"Coffee." Debbie spoke firmly. "We'll see what we can find out while we embrace the healing properties of caffeine and Janet's baking."

"I—" Sadie hesitated. She fiddled with her hair again and stood there in the center of the room, frowning.

"Come on." Janet touched Sadie's arm and gave her a soothing smile. "I solve puzzles better over coffee. Good cake only makes it that much easier."

CHAPTER SIX

Sadie had a single-serve brewing system in the small bedroom-turned-office. The former dining room was now a doll repair room. The home's living room was the storefront, flanked with displays of old dolls and some new favorites. Most of the old dolls were sweet, but Janet shuddered when she glimpsed a couple of the creepier ones. Dolls weren't her thing. But Sadie had developed a skill set for turning old and broken into fully functional, and a growing number of people appreciated that. Already, delivery trucks had dropped off seven new "patients" for her to repair.

"I'm on coffee," announced Debbie. She brewed three cups then added a fourth when Drew's car pulled up to the back side of the house.

Sadie tapped on the window to show him where they were, and after a moment he came into the office with a broad smile.

"Hello, all." He grinned and snagged a cupcake. "I didn't have time for lunch today. The ER was crazy with the increase in flu cases. So this"—he took a bite of the cupcake and sighed—"is real nice. Hey." He must have noticed Sadie's distress, because he bent closer. "You okay? What's up?"

Sadie took a deep breath. Janet half expected her to get emotional, but the breath seemed to steady her. She motioned for Drew to take a seat. When he did, she explained what had happened, and he scowled. "He threatened you?"

"No." She waved that off. "Although you could say he behaved in a threatening manner. He was angry and kept saying my family is a bunch of terrible people, when I know they're not." She paused and circled the rim of her coffee cup with one finger. "He waved around a picture of Gigi and Great-Grandpa Joe when they were much younger. Then he accused them of being traitors. And of shaking the dust of the Janek name off their German boots."

Drew's reaction was the same as Sadie's had been. "German boots? Where in the world did he get that?"

"Your guess is as good as mine," Sadie told him. "I might have been able to laugh it off and dismiss him as some nutcase, but he had that photo. One I've never seen. Where did he get it? What does he know that I don't, and why does this complete stranger get to know more about my family than I do? This is so frustrating!"

Janet saw Ian drive up in his cruiser. She tapped on the window, and Ian came in the same way Drew had.

Drew stood and shook Ian's hand.

Debbie motioned to the coffee maker, but Ian shook his head. "I've had too much already. So, Sadie." He pulled up a chair and settled across from Drew and Sadie. "The anonymous email, the brooch, and now this. Any two of those things could conceivably be coincidence." He spoke mildly, one of his gifts. Ian was able to put folks at ease because he was at ease. "Add the third, and we have to figure you've touched a nerve somewhere. Can I see the photo you posted on your website?"

Sadie picked up her phone, swiped the screen, and handed it to him. Ian studied it then passed it to Janet.

"The trunk is in this picture too," Janet said.

"I staged it that way on purpose," Sadie said. "The first image in the post is the doll on my dining room table. The ivory brocade made a great backdrop. But then I wanted one with the trunk, so I opened it and set the rag doll on the edge. I wanted to tie history with history."

"So this man's interest might have nothing to do with the doll and something to do with the trunk," Debbie suggested.

Sadie sat back, clearly surprised. "I didn't even consider that. I assumed it was about the doll because that email was about the doll."

Janet nodded. "I was thinking the same thing as Debbie. He didn't come in here yelling about the doll or the brooch, which probably means he doesn't even know they exist. He was angry about something else."

"Something to do with the family," Debbie said. "But what would have goaded him to come here now, out of the blue?"

"The trunk." Sadie breathed deep. "I never thought of that. But how could he recognize a trunk that came to this country so many decades ago?"

"He might not have recognized it, per se," suggested Janet. "But he's clearly upset with your family. Maybe seeing the trunk posted on your page sent him into a tailspin." She shrugged. "It's a relatively innocuous posting. But something got him riled up, and he never said a word about a doll. Just about family and traitors."

"What if he's right?" Sadie whispered the words in a half-strangled voice. "He said they had 'German boots.' What if we find out that my ancestors were traitors? History has uncovered a lot of treachery that went on during the two world wars. What if the Harpers were part of that deceit or cheating?"

Drew took her hand. "They were what they were, honey. We can't change the past. We can't undo it. We acknowledge it and get on with our lives like we've been doing all along. I don't care what your great-grandparents did or didn't do. They came here and started a new life once the shadows of war lifted. If they did something wrong, that's on them. Not us. We don't have to live in the shade of their actions. And we might be better off not knowing what they were," he added firmly.

Sadie shook her head. "I have to know. I've wondered for a long time why I couldn't delve into my family's past. I need to know why a simple post has gotten these weird reactions from two absolute strangers."

Drew pressed his lips together, clearly disagreeing.

She put her other hand on top of his. "We also need to think of the girls, Drew. We can't change their pasts or their ancestors' choices, but we can help them be strong enough to face the future. I'm a mom, first and foremost, and to suddenly have two strangers upset with me and my family makes me concerned for their safety. Maybe these people mean no harm. But we can't assume they're safe until we know for a fact that it's true. And if that's unreasonable, well then." She splayed her hands. "I'm being unreasonable."

"I'd say you're being wise," Ian said. "The more we know, the less we have to worry about."

"All right," Drew said. "As long as when all's said and done, I get to have a real serious discussion with the guy who barged in here and yelled at my wife."

Ian stood. "I understand you wanting to do that, Drew, but let me look into it once we figure out who he is before you talk to him. I don't want you walking into something dangerous. If this guy was simply spouting off in the heat of the moment, we don't want to make his life worse or push him over the edge." He leaned over to kiss Janet's cheek. "I'll see you at home. I swung by the house to let Laddie out a little bit ago, so if you take longer than you thought, he's all set."

He left through the side door, and Drew headed up to the attic to bring down the little dresser.

The women faced one another over the table. "We need to figure out who that man is," Janet announced.

"Yes, we do," Debbie agreed, "but we don't want to pour fuel on his fire. With Good Shepherd closed to visitors for a few more days, maybe we can put Annie and Joe on hold and try and figure out this guy—"

"And the anonymous email sender," Janet cut in.

"And what they have to do with me and my family." Sadie folded her arms across her chest.

Drew carried the small dresser down the stairs and wrestled it into the back seat of Debbie's car.

When they'd said goodbye and were back in the car, Janet thought for a moment and then said, "Do you think it really was the trunk that triggered that Janek guy?"

"Who knows?" Debbie backed out of the parking space. "I'm anxious to find out the reason behind all this. I know Ian said it could be a coincidence, but I think that two strangers coming out of the woodwork over a social media post is more than that. It's downright mysterious." She flashed a smile at Janet. "And that's where we come in."

"I never guessed that getting the café up and running would bring a side gig, but it seems we have a knack." Janet pulled out her phone to type in a few notes. "I'm pretty sure God's timing put us at this place and at this time for a reason. He knew all these mysteries and puzzles would come to the Whistle Stop Café." She smiled. "And I, for one, am perfectly fine with that."

Kielce, Poland
October 1940

Dearest Nessie,

I am concerned that I have not heard from you in so long.

My heart questions why no word has come, but then reason takes hold. With a world in turmoil, my words and your words are probably of small significance to others, and yet a part of me fears that people read our words and destroy them. Why anyone would tamper with the words of one beloved sister to another, I do not know, but when silence stretches so long, I wonder. And yes, I worry, but not for me.

God has me in His blessed hands. This I trust. This I know.

But I do worry for so many taken away from this beloved country, a country I've loved for so long. I see the trodden fields and the broken homes and places left to fall to rubble. The sadness is hard to endure. I knew many of these people, as did you. I talked with them. Walked with them. Worshiped with them and their children. The reality of their weather-beaten homes hits deep.

When you do write—when you can, dear sister— tell me of the land there.

Is it rich? Do fields grow thick and lush? Do trees hang ripe with fruit? I hear of mountains and valleys and rivers, and as I gaze upon our river here, I think of a time when all was well. Now the life-giving water is a boundary separating one conqueror from another, and it means so little in retrospect.

Some days I scold myself for doubting your wisdom. Why was I so shortsighted? Why didn't I trust you? Why didn't I grab Joseph's arm and insist we embrace a new beginning? But you know my husband. He isn't stubborn, but he is firm in his belief that a country is worth taking care of. Was it change I feared, or did taking a leap like you did seem like too much work? I—well, we—opted for the known over the unknown, and yet our safety and sovereignty were gone in short order. Looking back, I wonder over our choices and second-guess myself. But were they God's choices or ours?

That I cannot say.

Writing these missives makes me glad for Baba's insistence on our schooling at a time when girls were rarely instructed. She believed in developing mind and matter, and her generosity made that possible. Boarding school set us apart from others, and we saw the opportunities of life firsthand. How others lived. How things were done. Now I know how important it is for people to command multiple languages and customs. How wise Baba and Mama were to insist we attend the academy. It gave us an edge that might make a difference now. Two of the women I sew for speak some English. In that way we can communicate.

Most are kind to me, but one is not. For that one I remind myself of the greater good, and it helps, Nessie. It helps.

I remain your loving sister,

Anya

CHAPTER SEVEN

anet's mom greeted Janet and Debbie at her front door the
following afternoon. She swung the door wide as they dashed
up the steps in a cold, driving March rain. "Come on in!" she exclaimed
as they hurried onto the small porch. "Coffee and snacks await."

She'd laid out an assortment of cheese, crackers, pepperoni, and
olives with sides of grapes.

"Mom, you made a charcuterie board for us." Janet gave her a
quick hug. "That's so nice."

"It's a sensible kind of thing for folks who are around sweets all
day." Her mom tipped her gaze to the small box in Janet's hand.
"Although I'm pretty sure some of those sweets followed you here."

Janet set the box on the table and laughed as she peeled off her
heather-blue sweatshirt. "Guilty as charged."

"You need a raincoat," Mom scolded. "So you don't get soaked
to the skin. I do believe I got you one three years back."

"You did, and I love it. It's in the hall closet where it should be,
because it wasn't raining this morning," Janet pointed out.

Mom angled a pointed look toward the cute raincoat Debbie
had hung on the coat tree inside the door.

Janet laughed. "Debbie's always been more on top of wardrobe
choices than I have, and you know it. I tend to grab whatever's

handy when I hop into the car before dawn every morning. Although I am spoiled by the remote car start that Ian got for me. That's such a blessing all winter. And by the time you sent me the rain warning at the crack of dawn, I'd been baking for over an hour. No worries, Mom."

"I'm not inclined to worry, but March is fickle around here. History tells us that." Mom slid a chair in front of her open laptop. "Lots of people suffered in the flood of 1913, and every history buff I know recognizes that it could happen again. Although they did dismantle the canals, so things are different now. Still, a stalled system on saturated ground spells trouble."

"Was the flood really bad, Lorilee?" Debbie finished making a cup of tea from the one-cup brewer and then settled into a seat at the table.

"Dreadful," Mom told her. "Hundreds were lost in Ohio and several other states. Easter was early that year too, even earlier than this year, and it didn't stop raining for days. The storm took out houses and businesses and bridges, leaving a long path of destruction behind."

"How awful," Janet murmured.

"It was," Mom agreed. "My family had a farm about forty miles north of here. I haven't found much in our family history about the storm affecting them, but Steve's family was in New Philadelphia along what had been the Ohio and Erie Canal. They had three businesses not far from the waterway, and all three were ruined. They had no insurance, so they pooled their funds and started over. That was the beginning of the Hill's Grocery chain."

The family's small group of grocery stores had been sold to a regional grocer when Janet was in elementary school, but her father still had a HILL'S GROCERY sign hanging in the garage. The sign was pure nostalgia. He had worked stocking shelves during high school, but he had no interest in a retail career.

"I had no idea they went through all that." Janet watched the single-serve coffee maker pour hot water into her mug. "Mom, do you want tea?" she asked. "Or coffee?"

"I'll take a cup of tea," Mom replied. "I didn't know how tough things were either. I mean, I heard your father's grandmother talk about the hard times, and about her father and the uncles disagreeing over this, that, and the other thing, but it didn't click until I started doing genealogy research on the families. It's fascinating to learn what people endured and how they got through tough times."

"Does it really go into all that on an ancestry site?" asked Debbie.

Mom shook her head. "No. But people add links to their profiles, so you can put together a glimpse of what each time period brought. It makes it easier to launch an internet search. At minimum, it gives you somewhere to start."

"You didn't do enough research work as an editor?" Janet took a seat and handed her mom a cup of tea. Her mother had been a book editor at a Christian publishing house before her retirement a few years before. "Checking authors' facts up one side and down the other?"

"Nope." Mom's smile convinced Janet of her sincerity. "I loved it then, and I love it now." She rubbed her hands together. "So, who or what are we searching for?"

"The family name is Janek," Janet told her. "And Martin Janek is the name we're interested in." She'd gotten that info from Ian the night before, based on what he'd found from the license plate number she'd caught. "He's listed online in New Philadelphia, but we don't know how long he's been there. His family could have been anywhere, but let's try our area first."

"Spelling?" Mom's fingers hovered over the keyboard.

She typed the letters as Janet spelled the name for her. Then she frowned. "Nothing for Martin. Let's try the surname alone." She reentered the last name with better results. "There are Janeks in several census forms over the decades. Let me open a couple of those." She lifted her brows as she slid her reading glasses farther up her nose. "Well, someone has done some work already. Here's a family tree." She sat back so that Janet and Debbie could see the lineage.

Twenty minutes later, they had learned nothing that linked the Harpers to the Janeks.

Mom took her glasses off, rubbed her eyes, and sat back in her chair. "Why are we looking into this man and his family? Is there a concern?"

Janet took the lead. "He came into Sadie Flaherty's shop and called her family traitors. Naturally, that was upsetting. He seems angry about things that happened a long time ago, but we don't understand his investment in the situation."

Mom's brows shot up. "The Harpers? Traitors? They're about the nicest folks around. Mary Harper Stone used to work at Stutzman's General Store in Sugarcreek. My mother would drive up there to buy supplies in bulk. She and Mary exchanged recipes and family news over the years. I got to know Mary better years later when I frequented the store."

"I have a vague memory of the place," Janet said. "I remember the aisle with the bins of chocolate chips, brown sugar, and oats."

"It's still a wonderful place to buy in bulk," her mother said.

"So Mary didn't take to sewing the way Lena did?" Debbie asked.

Mom shrugged. "She helped now and then, but it wasn't her specialty. Not like Lena. Lena liked sewing and creating. The very thought that someone running a doll hospital could be a traitor is ridiculous."

Janet failed to see the correlation there. "I'm not sure what one has to do with the other."

"Character arcs." In Mom's world, everything came down to good, strong writing. "I worked with character arcs for decades, and even the best-kept secrets or personality traits will sneak out when least expected. My mother and I knew Mary from the store, and I went to church with Lena." She shrugged. "They aren't, and never were, traitors of any kind, and I'll stake my reputation on that."

"What if Martin is talking about something that happened before their time?" Debbie suggested. "Like during the war or even before that?"

Mom pursed her lips. "I can't speak to the Harper family as a whole, as I never met Mary's parents. But I can tell you that she and Lena didn't have a deceitful bone in their bodies, which in my experience usually means they were raised that way by good, upstanding people. So I don't have a clue what this Janek guy is talking about."

"Sadie said her grandmother mentioned some kind of relationship to the Janeks from long ago," Janet told her. "Mary refused to say more than that, though, and Sadie never asked. It didn't seem like a big deal at the time. But I don't see anywhere on this tree that links the Janeks to the Harpers. Do you, Mom?"

"No. Now that doesn't mean it isn't so," she reminded them. "Like anything else, this information is only as good as the person providing it."

Janet sat back, disappointed. "I was sure this would be the easy way to find out how Martin Janek is related to Sadie." She thought for a moment. "Maybe this means they're not related at all, and Martin is some random guy who came in and yelled about something he's gotten all wrong."

Her mother clicked back to the site's search screen. "Let's see if there's anything under the Harper side." She typed the surname and their geographic location.

Nothing came up.

She changed her keywords.

Still nothing came up linking the Harpers of Dennison and Uhrichsville with anyone.

Debbie folded her arms. "Is this normal?"

Mom shrugged. "Yes and no. Not every family has a member with the time to fill in the blanks, and the sites cost money to set up. But usually you'll see someone or something linked to a name. I see death certificates here." She indicated a flag on one side. "For Joseph and Annie Harper. And for Mary Harper Stone, for her husband, Brian Stone, and her brother, Michael Harper, but those come from links for an ad for another site. Not because anyone has entered them into this site's database."

Janet raised her eyebrows at Debbie, who nodded.

Mom noticed the exchange. "What are you two thinking?"

"That maybe there's a reason for no digital footprint." Janet bit her lip. "Sadie said she was going to do a genealogical profile for a college project, but her father told her that delving into the past or anything about their family around World War II could upset her grandmother. He advised Sadie to let them keep their secrets."

"Oh my." Mom minimized the site, closed the laptop, and folded her hands. "I'm not privy to whatever went on with the Harpers, but we all know there's no shortage of secrets in the aftermath of a war. People see, do, and hear unimaginable things—both soldiers in battle and civilians in hardship. I can't blame anyone for wanting to put the horrors of war behind them. It's self-protective and a way for a lot of people to handle the trauma."

"Except Ireland never joined the fight," Debbie pointed out. "They maintained as much neutrality as they could, although they weren't immune to being caught in the cross fire."

"Not taking sides can be more dangerous than declaring a side," Mom said. "A lot of people embrace the 'if you're not with us, you're against us' mindset. Also, Ireland had a thriving black market because of severe rationing. I know this because one of my authors did a deep dive into it when she was creating a World War II romance half a dozen years back."

"Black markets can be very dangerous," Janet murmured.

"And they might explain hidden jewels," Debbie added.

Mom's eyebrows shot up. "Jewels?"

"Sadie found a brooch hidden in an old rag doll in Lena's attic," Janet explained. "But what makes it really odd is that she didn't find the brooch right away. She posted the doll on her social media page, along with the trunk she found it in, and someone sent her an intimidating message about secrets inside the doll, and that he or she wanted the truth to finally come out. Sadie examined the rag doll and discovered the brooch. She'd never heard anything about a lost brooch, so she has no way of knowing who it belonged to or who put it inside the doll. Or why they hid it in the first place. Or if the person who hid it is the same person who wrote her, or if it's someone else altogether. If it is someone else, how do they know about it?"

Mom whistled softly. "My stars, that's beyond strange. I mean, way beyond."

"It sure is." Debbie pointed to the laptop. "That's why we hoped for some kind of clue there, between Martin Janek, Sadie, the brooch, and the doll—or at least the trunk. Although he didn't mention any of that to us. He just barged into the shop and started yelling."

"How would anyone know about the trunk?" her mother asked.

"Sadie posted a picture of the doll with the trunk to show where she'd found it. We thought it might be the trunk that lit a fire under Martin Janek because he didn't mention a word about the doll or the brooch, and it seems like he would have if that's what brought him raging into the doll shop. Don't you think?"

"I think you're right to investigate," Mom said. "People take secrets to their graves for a lot of reasons—personal, monetary, and sometimes criminal. War is a horrible time, and sometimes it pushes people to do things they'd never do in normal circumstances. I don't condemn anybody for that," she added. "I figure that's between them and God."

Janet stood and hugged her mother. "I should head home and get a few things done before Ian gets there. Thanks, Mom."

"Yes, thank you, Lorilee." Debbie hugged her too, from the other side. "We'll head out so you can get back to your tree building. And my mom said to tell you she's impressed by what you're doing and wants to do the same thing. She's always wanted to do a genealogy page but never had the time when she was working full-time. She's excited that she's got time now, especially before spring hits."

"I'll call her," Mom promised. "We can get together and talk."

"Perfect."

Janet and Debbie headed out.

The rain hadn't stopped. If anything, it came down harder, and the wind whipped sheets of water up onto the porch. Janet eyed the rain, then her friend. "I'm not waiting. I'm making a run for it."

Debbie chuckled. "Me too."

They tugged up their hoods, dashed to their cars, and climbed in quickly before going their separate ways. As she rounded a corner, Janet weighed what they'd learned.

They'd found nothing to link the Janeks to the Harpers. That was unfortunate.

But maybe more importantly, they'd found nothing to link the Harpers to anyone. That in itself was a red flag. Ancestry sites had been around for over two decades. The likelihood of no one linking to the Harper family in Dennison wasn't just unusual. Janet was pretty sure it was nearly impossible, and that was something to check into.

From the Diary of Anya Oleski

Poland
November 1940

I am living a lie.

I know this to be true, I am understanding of the choices, and yet, with our conditions for living, my options are thin. It is not my normal nature to shade truths, but when one is surrounded by foreign soldiers and their wives, it is, perhaps, the lone option. With Marysia gone and Joseph conscribed to working the railroad under German control, there is so little I can say, do, or even be.

The churches are closed.

So many people have been taken away. Untold numbers, sent off to no one knows where. I am allowed to stay because I carry Baba and Mama's gift in my fingers. A prominent woman has discovered my talent and hired me to alter her gowns to accommodate her delicate condition. I cannot say no, lest I become a martyr for a turned hem, and yet the fear is that it will seem I approve of what is happening. I don't. I abhor it. To be Marysia's mother I must stay alive, and yet I hate myself for allowing others to use me in such a way as this.

Is it cowardice that keeps me sewing?

I cannot say it isn't, but if I can balance the "must do" with what I can do, I will offer it up to God as penance. He alone is my guide. He alone is my salvation.

I do what is needed and help where I can, but it is an odd situation all around. My English schooling holds me in good stead.

Evil surrounds me even as I write this.

God help us, for only He can inspire what must happen to regain our freedom to live and love again.

It is a country shadowed in the darkest cloud.

Lord, bring the sun again. Please.

CHAPTER EIGHT

Green, swirled frosting, mint-flavored chocolate, and a tub of Celtic-themed sprinkles added a dash of Irish fun to Janet's baking on Monday, but an early Easter meant she also needed pastel sprinkles and adornments for a quick switch over to pastels on March nineteenth to celebrate the first official day of spring. St. Patrick's Day—and, incidentally, Tiffany's birthday—was on Sunday, so the café was hosting a spring kickoff event with a Celtic-themed pair of Doughnut Days on Friday and Saturday. They would draw a crowd with their outdoor doughnut frying, which would help their bottom line and benefit the depot museum.

She'd hoped Tiffany would be home for spring break, but those plans had changed when Tiffany and two friends had decided to take a short trip to Manhattan. Janet had to remind herself—several times, actually—that her daughter was old enough to go on a road trip with her friends. She'd be home on Wednesday, and they'd have time to celebrate her nineteenth birthday on Sunday before taking her back to the dorms at Case Western in Cleveland. When she texted Tiffany about what she'd like for her birthday, the answer came back immediately. STEAK ON THE GRILL AND CREAM PUFFS. NO CAKE. NOTHING BEATS YOUR CREAM PUFFS, MOM. I'M NOT SURPRISED THAT PEOPLE ORDER THEM ALL THE TIME.

It was true. The chocolate-frosted, cream-filled pastries were a huge hit and easy to prepare now that she'd nailed down her choux technique, so their rising popularity was a blessing to the café's receipts.

Janet's father, Steve, called shortly after the café opened at seven. "The weather might be dicey for Doughnut Days."

Janet had checked the forecast too. "Mother Nature could put a damper on things. Our little pop-up tents won't hold under a strong wind. I'm hoping the long-term forecast is wrong, but we'll need to have a Plan B."

"I've got two ideas," her dad said. "Your mom and I have been talking about buying a tent—a big, sturdy one that'll handle all kinds of weather. I've got room in the garage rafters to store it. You could use it for the café whenever you want."

It was a lovely idea, but Janet and Debbie had priced the heavy-duty tents the previous fall and decided their fledgling business would have to struggle along without one for a while. "They're kind of expensive, Dad."

"Not so bad if you figure we'd be using it for years," he replied. As a longtime accountant, Janet's dad was always quick to examine the cost-per-year ratio on purchases. "It's a twofold investment, from the café's perspective. A sturdy canvas tent can be an umbrella during rain or snow, and shade in summer. We'd be fine with family and friends using it too. We think it makes sense. The other idea is to move Doughnut Days to under the front overhang facing the road. Like in that Salvation Army photo from World War II, with the women handing out doughnuts to soldiers."

Janet loved that old photo. "I really like the idea of recreating that picture. It would make a great advertisement to promote Doughnut Days, but we can't set up there. If a storm comes in from the north or northwest, we'll get pelted. From that perspective, the tent idea is better, but I don't want you spending money."

Her father scoffed at her objection. "What better reason to spend money? Can't take it with me," he quipped, and he sounded truly delighted. "I'll put the order in, and maybe we can stage a picture in front of the depot this summer when the weather is more cooperative. Then we could post both photos side-by-side."

"That's a great idea," Janet said. "Thanks, Dad."

A few minutes later Debbie was taking orders from their first customers of the day when Harry crossed the parking lot between the café and the gazebo. The weekend's rain had paused, but the day was still blustery, cold, and damp. Janet opened the door for Harry, but he didn't come in. "I stopped by to get my order to go," he told her. "The weather has Crosby feeling a little down and out, and I'm not much better myself, so I figured I'd walk over and take a bite back with me. Scrambled eggs, please, if you don't mind. With rye toast."

Harry's house was around the corner and not a long walk at all, but he was clearly tired today. And for him to come over without Crosby worried Janet. "Harry, come in out of the cold. I don't want you standing out there like that. And you can always call us with an order. We'd gladly run it over to your place."

"I'll call next time." He jutted his chin toward the open door. "That's a mighty nice offer, to run it by our place, and I don't mind a delivery fee. But I'll wait out here today. I don't want to be sharing germs with anyone."

"You'll do no such thing," Janet assured him. "You go on home and get comfy and warm, and I'll run your order over in five minutes. Maybe six," she amended with a smile.

Harry protested one more time then proved how awful he felt by obeying her. Janet made toast, scrambled some eggs, and boxed it all up. She set the timer for her peppermint-swirl loaves before heading out.

She knocked on Harry's door and was surprised not to hear Crosby's answering bark. The mixed-breed dog, a descendant of Dennison's famous World War I service dog, Bing, was always ready to greet people. His silence sent up a red flag.

"Door's open," Harry called.

Janet hurried into the kitchen. It was cramped but clean—typical Harry—and perfect for a bachelor. As a longtime train conductor, he was accustomed to small work areas, so the size of the house didn't bother him. Janet set the to-go containers onto the table. "There you go, my friend. What's the matter with Crosby?"

Harry frowned. "I don't know. He's off his feed and seems tired and a little anxious. It started a day or two ago, and it's getting worse." His voice caught. He swallowed hard and stared down at his cherished friend. "Whatever it is, it's come on him suddenly. Nothing I would expect for a dog his age."

Janet bent and peered into Crosby's eyes.

He appeared as worried as his owner. She rubbed his ears, set his egg and toast in front of him, and stood back up. "Would it be okay if I have Ian get ahold of Dr. Kendall?" Heidi Kendall was the local veterinarian, an amazing woman with a real knack for animal care. Janet would call her, but Crosby was too big for her to handle if he needed to be carried. Ian could arrange an appointment that would fit his schedule.

"I'd appreciate it," Harry replied. "I can't get him there myself, so if Ian wouldn't mind, that would be an answer to my prayer."

Janet watched as Crosby sniffed at his food then laid his head back on his paws. "I'll call him this morning. And I'll have soup and a sandwich dropped off for lunch. You stay here, out of the wind, and get better. All right?"

Harry looked relieved. "I'd be grateful, for certain." He reached into his pocket. "You tell me what I owe, and I'll—"

"We've got it covered, Harry." She crossed to the door as she spoke. "You concentrate on getting well. Okay?"

He nodded and tried to smile, but she could still see the concern in his eyes. Janet was pretty sure that Crosby's issues had Harry more worried than he cared to let on. "That'll be my focus. For both of us. At my age, I know time is running on the short side, but my little buddy isn't an old dog. It pains me to see him acting like one."

"Let's not borrow trouble," Janet said. "We'll wait and see what Dr. Kendall says."

She got back to the café in time to take the sweet breads out of the oven. Then she whipped up some cookie batter and called Ian.

"I'll call Heidi right away," he told her. "And I'll take Crosby for whatever time slot they give me. If I'm tied up, I'll see if Greg can do it." Greg Connor was finishing a bathroom renovation for their next-door neighbor. "How bad is he?"

Janet didn't like the answer to his question. "Bad, I think. He's like a different dog. He didn't greet me at the door, and he had no appetite, even for scrambled eggs. He just looks plain sad, Ian, and you know that's not Crosby's nature."

"I'll let Heidi know."

"Thank you."

Debbie had been listening to Janet's end of the conversation. When Janet explained that Greg might step in to take the dog to the veterinarian, Debbie said, "Greg and Harry both love our grilled chicken-salad sandwiches. I was going to make it for tomorrow, but I think today is better. I should have some time to do that later this morning."

Janet didn't miss the worry on Debbie's face, and she knew it was mirrored on her own. Harry had been relatively healthy for a man his age, and everyone who knew him credited Crosby for much of that. She hated to think of how her elderly friend would cope if something happened to his best friend.

The café was busy most of the morning, but when she got a moment, Janet texted Sadie. CAN WE MEET LATER TODAY?

Sadie texted back immediately. NOT TODAY. GIRLS HAVE DANCE, THEN VIOLIN. SOCCER TOMORROW, BUT I CAN DROP THEM OFF AND HAVE NINETY MINUTES FREE. DOES THAT WORK? AROUND 3:45?

PERFECT, Janet texted. WE'LL STOP BY. HOUSE OR DOLL HOSPITAL?

DOLL HOSPITAL.

Janet typed in IT'S A DATE and got back to frosting more cupcakes.

Ian called Janet about five minutes later. "Hey, I was able to get Crosby an appointment for one thirty. I have a meeting then, but

Greg's going to take him. I stopped by to let Harry know. You're right—neither one of them is acting like himself."

"I know." Janet choked back a rise of emotion. "It's been upsetting me all morning."

"We'll get it checked out," Ian promised. "If we get Crosby squared away, Harry will likely follow. I think he's mostly worried about the pooch."

Ian's Scottish mother had always referred to dogs as "pooches," and every now and again, Ian did the same. "I agree. Thank you, honey."

"Glad to help. See you tonight."

Janet shared the updates with Debbie. When she repeated what Ian had said about Harry, Debbie sighed. "We need to get those two back up to snuff." She mixed chicken with freshly chopped celery and walnuts. "We're going to pray this is a passing thing and that a few days of tender loving care will set things right."

Janet smiled. "Agreed. And—"

Her phone rang. Sadie's name came up on the display, and Janet swiped to accept the call. "What's up, Sadie?"

"Estelle Parkins just stopped by."

The name was familiar to Janet, but she couldn't recall meeting Estelle. "I don't know who that is, Sadie."

"She lives across the street and up a couple of houses from the doll hospital," Sadie told her. "She and Aunt Lena were close friends. They'd have tea together nearly every day during the slower times here. Aunt Lena thought the world of her, and Estelle took her death really hard. Estelle is quite the seamstress. She could whip up period-style doll clothes in a few hours, and never asked for a penny other than material costs. She simply loved helping."

"She sounds marvelous."

"She is," Sadie replied. "Some of our neighbors tried to stir up trouble when Aunt Lena left the business and house to me. They said Estelle had put in a lot of time to get nothing in return. I've kind of shied away from her since taking over because what if she really does feel that way? I've been afraid to talk to her, but she sounded fine about it a few minutes ago."

Janet considered that as she packaged small trays of a dozen cookies each for an order. "Funerals and wills can heal old wounds and open new ones. It's nice to hear she sounded all right."

"Exactly," agreed Sadie. "But she said something weird when she was here, and I had to call and tell you."

That piqued Janet's interest. "What was it?"

"She called Aunt Lena the 'product of jewels,'" Sadie said. "I didn't say anything or ask her why she said that, but ever since I found the brooch, everything seems to have a hidden meaning."

"It's always that way when you're trying to solve a mystery," Janet said. "You tend to open every door, even when you know the rooms are empty. But it is an odd turn of phrase, isn't it? 'Product of jewels.'"

"It sure is," Sadie agreed. "I can't even imagine what it means."

"Then we'll ask her," Janet reasoned. "See if she can come over and meet with us tomorrow. Sometimes a frank discussion offers the best explanation. And if it doesn't, it might give us a direction to go in."

"Okay," said Sadie. "I'll give her a call. What could it hurt?"

From the Diary of Anya Oleski

Poland
August 1941

If my beloved knew of these musings, he would burn them.

He knows the power wielded over us. He sees much, but the few times that he is here, in what we once called home, he is pensive and on guard. To be so limited in what he can do to help others wears on him, much as it does on me.

Yet we move forward, a couple in love, a couple with one blessed child safely tucked away. We cannot see her, but each time we think of our Marysia, we bless the Lord for keeping her safe. If we have nothing else, that is enough.

How we wish that the same could be said for all children.

I had two appointments today, new women in need of gowns as they take over some of the finer homes in our town.

People of prominence have been spirited away. And farmers—those who had acres of good, fertile land—have been made to leave. It is said that Germans will settle here and own the land. And although the Russians held ground across the river long enough to exile many of our people to the vast northern waste-land, they put their trust in the wrong place, for Germany has taken over the Eastern lands and sent Russia running.

What form of insanity is this?

None I can explain, but men with power and weap-ons can be the most dangerous sort if their hearts are not of God. And this is what we face now. It is useless to lament the unwise choices of a younger Anya and Joseph. For now, we look forward and help others as we can.

The streets have grown empty. It is only the poor folk who remain and those with skilled labor like Joseph and, by chance, myself.

I have decided to continue the practice of piec-ing blankets, because the officers' wives are leaving scraps with me. Much can be done with bits of this and that. The blankets can be sent to where they are needed to keep others snug and warm. My dear ones in Lisbon are ever grateful, and they treasure the work of my hands with each transport. They under-stand the gravity of our situation and our task, and they respect both. To them, I send a true blessing.

Joseph will get the newest creation to the post near Hungary, and from there it will go to Portugal with God's benevolence.

And may He, the King of kings, bless the works of my hands and those of my beloved.

CHAPTER NINE

anet finished packaging the five dozen cookies. She slipped the last *Whistle Stop Café* label into place as the ladies guild chairwoman stepped inside to pick them up. Violet Lincoln's smile lit up the room as she paid for the cookies. "We're giving a dozen to each person on the church staff," she told Janet. "Pastor Nick and the rest of the crew go the distance for us all year. They get inundated with remembrances at Christmas, but that's about it for the year. We decided we'd make sure there was a gift of thanks to them every season from now on, because Faith Community Church has been a help to so many for a long time."

"What a wonderful idea," Janet said. "Pastor Nick shows up at everything from baseball games to community fundraisers, and we appreciate that." She handed the bagged cookies to Violet. "Thank you for thinking of this. It's wonderful."

Violet beamed. "We thought so too. That man has counseled a lot of people through hard times. He's sat at many bedsides and held lots of hands throughout his years here. You'd think it would weigh heavy on a person to attend that many deaths, but his faith holds him up. He's a good man, all told."

"Absolutely," Janet agreed, then waved as Violet headed out the door. Her words set Janet thinking. Paulette Connor—Greg's mother, who worked for them part-time and was every bit as generous and helpful as her son—was busy with a few tables, which meant Janet could have a quick, private conversation. Janet moved closer to Debbie, who was packing a to-go order, and spoke in a low voice. "We could talk to Pastor Nick."

Debbie ladled soup into a container. "You mean about the Harpers and the Janeks?"

"He's been around long enough and helped enough families through grief that he might have an idea about all that. He might even know the secret that Sadie's grandmother Mary wouldn't tell anyone."

Debbie frowned. "You seriously want to ask a minister about what people might have told him in confidence?"

"Well, not exactly," Janet said. "But not everything he knows is confidential. And he's so fair-minded. He would never reveal something he shouldn't, but he may have some background information that could help."

Debbie wrinkled her nose. "I suppose that could be a last resort, if we absolutely can't come up with answers any other way. And I mean a *very* last resort."

Janet had to admit her friend was right. They wouldn't want Pastor Nick to break a confidence.

As Debbie finished bagging the to-go order, Greg Conner came through the door. Debbie caught sight of him and smiled.

So did he. And he kept smiling as he crossed the small dining area. "I love your chicken salad. I'm always glad to see it."

Somehow, Janet thought he meant he was always glad to see Debbie, but she kept the idea to herself.

"It's one of Harry's favorites," Debbie replied, but Janet didn't miss the twinkle in her eye. "And maybe I made it because you're going all out to help an elderly man and his dog."

Greg shrugged. "It's the right thing to do. Soup too?"

"Yes, to warm him up against this awful weather. And dog treats for Hammer and Crosby."

"Peanut butter?"

Her smile grew. "That's right. And maybe a couple of the human variety for you and Harry."

He pulled out his wallet to pay, but she waved him off. "This is on the house today. You get the Good Samaritan discount." She handed the bag to him.

He took it, closing his hand over hers for a moment longer than strictly necessary.

Her smile deepened. "Thank you, Greg. We all appreciate it."

"Happy to do it, ma'am." He grinned, and a tinge of color appeared in Debbie's cheeks. "I'll call later when we know more."

"We'd be grateful," Debbie told him. "We're both worried."

"I know. That's because you're good people." He headed out.

Janet nudged Debbie. "How did he know you made the chicken salad?"

"I texted him."

"I see." Janet stretched out the sentence.

Debbie avoided her gaze. "He's doing a good thing, and I wanted to do something special for him."

"Very thoughtful of you." Janet didn't bother trying to hide the knowing smile on her face.

"It's this town. I didn't see a lot of this kind of thing in my Cleveland office." Debbie put the salad container back in the refrigerated case. "Everyone was too busy to stop and help someone else, it seemed. So being part of Dennison again is kind of rejuvenating. Know what I mean?"

"I do. There were times when I was a little envious of your life in Cleveland," Janet confessed. "Not that I ever wanted to leave Dennison. I love this town, but our lives can seem dull and ordinary compared to life in the big city." She set the remaining cookie tray in the bakery case as Paulette came their way with her order pad and an almost empty coffeepot. "Then I got a little older and realized this place isn't ordinary at all. It's extraordinary and a great place to be. All of which makes me so glad you're here, that we're doing this together. That makes it even more special."

Paulette set the coffeepot on its base beside the espresso machine. "Speaking of specials, I need two chicken salads with lettuce, one on white toast and the other on a roll. Sweet potato fries with each. And don't think badly of me, but I couldn't help overhearing your discussion about Sadie's grandmother. You two should talk to Violet."

Janet raised a brow at her. "Why's that?"

"She was on the Helping Hands committee when Sadie's grandmother, Mary, took sick. She went to see her nearly every day toward the end. Violet and Sadie's mom were friends, and Violet was about the only person Mary would allow in to help her. Mary was a person who liked her privacy," Paulette explained.

"Interesting," Debbie murmured.

"I didn't know her personally. I remember folks saying she came by her passion for privacy honestly, though, because her mother, Annie Harper, was even more of a homebody. You didn't see her out much, except in her gardens. They grew all kinds of things behind the house. Of course, she'd had a farm in Ireland, so growing things was part of her nature. I remember hearing Mary say that all she remembered about the farm was how much her mother loved it."

Janet went back to the kitchen and weighed Paulette's words as she mixed up dough and batter for the next day's treats.

By the time they had flipped over the Closed sign and cleaned up, it was nearly three. Paulette had gone home a little past one, but Janet brought up her thoughts to Debbie. "You heard what Paulette said earlier, right? About Mary not being particularly outgoing?"

"And how that's the direct opposite of the way your mother described her relationship with Mary at the Amish store in Sugarcreek."

"Yes." Janet set out the pans she'd need first thing in the morning, along with four pounds of butter to soften overnight. "Can both be true? Or is one wrong?"

"I don't know." Debbie spoke slowly, considering the question. "It could be as simple as varying perspectives. You know, is the glass half-full or half-empty? That kind of thing."

"Valid point. We need to talk to more people."

"We do. Starting tomorrow, with Sadie and Estelle."

"Speaking of which," Janet said, "would you pick me up at my house tomorrow, and we can go to Sadie's together? I need to go home right after we close, and you can come get me when you and Paulette are done cleaning up."

"I can do that," Debbie said. "We should be done in plenty of time." She jutted her chin toward the phone in Janet's hand. "And by the way, that's about the tenth time you've checked that thing in the past thirty minutes."

"I know." Janet frowned. "I can't help wondering what's going on with Crosby. I haven't heard anything." She swiped at the screen a couple of times. "But on the bright side, Tiffany sent me a few pics from Liberty Island. She says they're having a ton of fun." She held out the phone for Debbie to see.

Debbie shook her head. "I don't know if I would have braved the island with that wind, but they seem happy. I remember a few fun trips of our own, Janet."

They exchanged smiles, and Janet checked her notifications again. "I sure wish we'd hear something," she said. "I'm really concerned about Crosby. And Harry."

"I know." Debbie wrung out the dishcloths and towels she took home and washed regularly to save on a laundry service. "I keep checking too. Maybe Heidi's running late."

Janet hoped that was it.

"Let's go sit with Harry," suggested Debbie.

"That's a great idea," Janet said. "We'll take him some cookies." She texted Ian, and then they walked up the road and knocked on Harry's door.

No answer.

Janet knocked again, harder this time. Harry's hearing wasn't the best. Crosby usually solved that problem by raising a ruckus when anyone came to the door. But Crosby wasn't there.

Still no response.

She exchanged a glance with Debbie then peered through the living room window. A chair blocked her view. Harry had once told her that he didn't spend time gazing out the front windows of his house. He preferred the view from a rear bedroom, where he could keep an eye on the comings and goings of the depot. A few years before, he'd had Ian and Janet move his favorite chair to that spot.

"Let's go around back," Debbie suggested.

They came around, and there was Harry, sitting by the window. He spotted them and waved for them to come in.

Debbie went in first, and Janet followed. Janet paused when she saw the sheen of tears in Harry's eyes.

Janet stepped forward and took his hand. "Harry, what is it? Have you heard something?"

A tear snaked its way down his weathered cheek. "No, nothing yet. I'm thinking of all the good times I've had and all the memories the Good Lord has given me. And how unfair it would be to cut a young dog's life short and leave an old codger like me hanging around."

Janet gave him a hug.

Debbie was more practical. "I call that borrowing trouble, Harry Franklin. You should know better." She scolded him gently as they moved into the kitchen, where she put his teakettle on the stove. "We don't know anything yet. I think a nice cup of tea with honey is the best thing for all of us. The tea soothes the nerves, and the honey soothes the throat. Janet and I are going to wait with you until we hear something," she went on. "Is that all right?"

Her words straightened his shoulders some. "I think that would be nice."

"And maybe a game of checkers?" Janet asked. "Although I never win because I don't strategize. I talk."

A ghost of a smile softened Harry's features. "I have heard Chief Ian say something of the sort."

Janet grinned. "I don't care about winning or losing. I like being with my family and friends. Are you a checkers shark, Harry?"

"I can hold my own," he replied with a twinkle in his eye.

"Then Debbie gets first game because she's better than me," Janet replied. "I brought some cookies for your cookie jar, and I'll set the kitchen to rights while you two play. If that's okay with you?"

"I would really appreciate that," he said. "Patricia came by last night after work to check on us, but I haven't had the strength to do much today."

"A cold will do that to you." Debbie took a seat across the small table from Harry then indicated the view out the kitchen window. "You can see the depot from here."

"First thing I noticed when I checked out this house. I couldn't do the stairs at our big house anymore, and it seemed like a waste of space and money to keep heating the place just for Crosby and me. Patricia and I hunted around, and we found this," he explained as he set the red discs in their proper places. "The price was right, and it's close to the trains and the depot. It was different once the trains stopped running, but that old train station is like home to me. And you gals moving a business in there has given Crosby and me a place to talk to people every day. We love sitting on our bench and watching the trains go by, but a good cup of joe and a bite taken in good company"—he smiled at them—"that's something to wake up to every morning."

"Did you fence the yard because you had Crosby?" Janet asked as she waited for the teakettle to sing.

Harry shook his head. "It was already there. Crosby wasn't but a pup when I first laid eyes on him. Maybe three months old, give or take, the doc said. He was begging a bite up and down the road, scavenging through garbage cans and making a nuisance of himself. He was skittish around people, like when a dog's never been loved by folks, you know? Nobody gave him much attention, but something about that dog spoke to me. Well, eventually I got him to come up on my front porch and have some food. After that he'd come in the house now and again for a quick visit. And then he decided he liked it inside this little house. It's been like that ever since. We have our walks and our rests, and we've lived that way for nearly seven years. Him and me, hanging about together."

"How did you find out he was related to Bing?" Debbie asked.

Harry exchanged a smile with Janet and said, "Janet and a few others sent one of those sample things into a DNA place, and they found markers that linked him to Bing. Not from Bing himself, of course, but from dogs they knew were related to him. I knew it before all that, though, because Crosby is special, like Bing was special. They're in for the long haul, if you get my drift."

"I do," Janet said.

"Me too," Debbie agreed. Her phone rang.

Debbie tapped her screen to accept the call. "Greg, hey. What's up? How are things going?" Then her face broke into a big smile, and she put the phone on speaker mode.

"It's a bad tooth, Harry." Greg stayed calm, but it would be impossible to miss the joyful note in his voice. "Tough for Crosby, but Doctor Kendall says she can extract it later today and he should be fine to come home tomorrow. He'll be right as rain."

"A tooth?" The relief in Harry's tone was heightened as he swiped a hand across his eyes. "Well then."

"I say we celebrate with a few of these cookies." Janet lifted the small box she'd brought over from the bakery. "Tea and cookies to celebrate our friend's healing."

"I didn't feel like eating much at all before this," Harry said. "But I wouldn't say no to a cookie. And a cup of tea."

Debbie beamed. "Greg, thank you so much for getting him over there."

"Listen to me, forgetting my manners." Harry smiled, and even though he still had a cold, he seemed so much better than he'd been even a few minutes earlier. "Thank you, Greg. You're a good friend."

"Happy to help. You know that, Harry. I'm leaving Crosby in good hands, and I'll pick him up on my lunch break tomorrow. Does that work for you?"

"It does. I'll make him some of that chicken soup he likes so much. That'll be something nice to come home to."

"It sure will. See you all later."

"Thanks again, Greg." Debbie ended the call.

Janet put a handful of cookies on a small plate, took them over to the table, and sat down next to Debbie. "Harry, that phone call is a big relief to all of us."

"It sure is," he replied.

"We're going to run your breakfast to you tomorrow morning, all right? That will give you another day to sit back and relax and fight off this bug. And if you need anything," she reminded him as she took a cookie from the plate, "you call us, all right?"

"I don't expect I'll need to." His tone almost sang with relief, and his worried expression had disappeared with Greg's phone call. "Knowing my furry friend is going to be all right is the best medicine I could have. Beating Debbie at checkers will put the frosting on the cake."

Debbie laughed and pretended to roll up her sleeves. "Don't count on it, Harry. I might be nice most of the time, but I'm ruthless at checkers, so let the games begin."

He laughed. Sometime later, when he won, he said, "Debbie, it does my old heart good to sit and have a game of checkers now and again. I thank you."

Debbie touched the back of his hand as she stood. "My pleasure, Harry. I'll see you in the morning."

The women went out the front door and strolled toward their parking spaces on the far end of the depot. The off-and-on rain had paused, but a gust of wind flapped white slips of paper on their windshields.

"What on earth?" Debbie reached her car first. "Who would put out flyers on a day like this? It's—" She stopped speaking as she read the message out loud. "'You might want to think about who you hang out with.'"

"Mine's the same." Janet gazed at Debbie over the hood of her car. "Martin Janek?"

"Maybe," Debbie said. "But why?"

Janet reread the note as if it would explain. "It's not like he's a customer here. He's never met us. The internet listed his address in

New Philadelphia, so why would he be angry with us? And how would he know these are our cars? It makes no sense. And is this person even talking about Sadie, or are we assuming that's the case?"

Debbie rubbed her temples. "I don't know, but it's cold, and things like this make me angry. I'm going home to calm down and think this through. What this person doesn't know is that being warned off doesn't work on us. It only makes us want to try harder. See you in the morning." She clutched the note as she settled into the driver's seat.

When Janet got home, she took her note inside and set it on the table.

Martin Janek was the lone suspect they had at the moment. But it couldn't be him, could it?

Kielce, Poland
August 1941

Dear Nessie,

When the winter hung on overlong, I prayed for warmer weather to come. I wanted spring, then summer. A chance to sow and weed, hoe and harrow, even if it was on less ground, but my work is for naught.

The garden we tended and groomed has been confiscated for others' use.

My harvest has been taken, and when that was done, I was given the promise that the late vegetables will be commandeered as well.

My heart grows tight at the thought.

Our beloved grandparents created that garden. They fed it each year, sweetening the soil with nature's nutrients. They were farmers of old with the wisdom of ages. They knew to rotate fields, to avoid inclines when possible, and to take work seriously, every day. We learned so much from them. You and I tended that garden with Mama and Papa, and we increased the size to help provide for Uncle Ludwig's family when he lost his plot of land. We toiled with our cousins at our side, working, laughing, and complaining because the river called to us. And yet work came first.

Joseph has found a source of food for us. For me, actually, because he is gone so often and there is food for him at the depots. Guilt consumes him because I am left here alone, and he worries for the surroundings. But no one bothers me. I think that is because I work for the wives of commanders and the wives have some influence with the men. They ensure that their seamstress lives unbothered.

I don't try to explain the unfairness of that. I live as I believe God would have me live. Some would say I work for the enemy, and they would not be wrong, but I know the simple truth: I work to survive, to get to where my heart lies, where I belong. God willing that will happen someday. For now, they leave me in peace—aside from confiscating the food I've worked so hard to grow.

To my favor, I shall never grow old and fat at this rate, and I've learned well that enough is truly enough. Sometimes, when I recall the days of plenty, it seems like a faraway dream.

My reality is to stay true to my work, my God, and my cause.

Our little darling comes to visit before the next term begins, although she is not so little now. I await her with open arms, for this is what keeps me strong. Her time here will be short, but blessed. And so it goes.

Praying for you and whatever you may be facing at your home and in your town. I would love to hear of it, but letters don't seem to be coming through if you are writing.

Go with God, dear sister. Go with God.

Your loving sister,

Anya

CHAPTER TEN

Janet's phone rang as she rode with Debbie to the doll hospital the next afternoon. She answered and hit the speaker button. "Hey, Sadie. We're on our way."

"The doll's gone, Janet."

Janet shot straight up in her seat and exchanged a look with Debbie, whose eyes were wide. "What?"

"Ian just left. I called him first thing when I realized it was missing. I came over early to get a few things done. Estelle had asked to see the doll this afternoon, and I said yes, of course. She's going to arrive any second, and it's gone."

Janet went straight into policeman's wife mode. "Was the door jimmied? Damaged? Was the house locked up tight? What did Ian say?"

"Yes, it was all locked up, and nothing was damaged or out of place. Ian couldn't see any signs of forced entry, so how did the person get in?" Sadie's voice quivered. "I can't even imagine. The doll was right there on the mantel over the old fireplace, and now it's gone."

"We're about to pull in," Janet replied. "We'll figure this out, Sadie. See you in a minute."

She and Debbie hurried to the side door and let themselves in, but Janet stopped Debbie as soon as they got through the door. She took out her phone, switched on the flashlight, and studied the stairway. At least two distinct sets of footprints went up the stairs, but that didn't offer much information, since one of them was probably Sadie's and the other Ian's.

Sadie hurried in. "I'm so glad you're here. I can't believe all the stuff that's happening. And here I thought inheriting this place was like a dream come true. It made it possible for me to do two things I love—doll restoration and sewing." She wrung her hands. "Aunt Lena never had this kind of trouble when she was in charge. Why now? Why me?"

"Sadie, how could someone get in?" Debbie asked. "Wasn't everything locked up tight?"

"I have no idea," Sadie insisted.

The side door opened again, and a woman came up the stairs. She wasn't what Janet had expected. Estelle must be in her mid-seventies, but she looked a decade younger.

Debbie reached to shake her hand. "Hi. I'm Debbie Albright. Janet and I went to school with Sadie."

"Why, I know the two of you from the café!" Estelle's voice chirped like a spring bird. "It takes me back a bit, let me tell you. Not to the war, of course, but to hearing my mama's stories about the war. That was something Lena and I had in common." She slipped off her coat and slung it onto the oak coat-tree. "We had stories to share and plenty of time to share them as we worked. Once I retired from writing greeting card sentiments, I helped with the sewing over here." She smiled brightly at Janet and Debbie then grasped Sadie's hand. "It was a labor of love to work with Lena Harper. Now, where is this doll you told me about?"

Sadie made a face. "Gone."

Surprise lifted Estelle's eyebrows. "Gone?"

Sadie nodded. "I'm afraid so. I had her on the old mantel, but she's not there anymore, and I can't imagine how, because nothing was jimmied open or broken, so how could anyone get in?"

Estelle made a wry face. "Perhaps the spare key beneath the That's My Baby rock?"

Sadie gaped at her. "The what?"

"I don't expect it's been used in a while, because you have your own key," Estelle said. "Your aunt kept a spare under the rock in case she forgot hers. If someone had to get into the house while she was gone, she'd tell them where the key was hidden."

"She told people where it was?" Janet loved living in a small town, but Lena letting people know where she kept her spare key was a bad idea no matter where she lived.

"Well, she wasn't much on changing her ways," Estelle said. "And she got more and more forgetful as the years went on. But then, she said she'd been a little forgetful all her life. She was forever putting things in 'safe places' and never seeing them again."

"That was Aunt Lena," Sadie agreed as Janet ducked back out the side door. Sure enough, a key lay under the stone that had been decorated with the business's name, a spray of flowers, and the image of a sweet old-fashioned doll.

She didn't touch the key with her bare hands. She went back inside. "Sadie, do you have a plastic storage bag and a paper towel?"

"Of course." Sadie left and returned a moment later with the requested items, and when Janet came back in with the key in the plastic bag, Sadie shivered. "It's like a real crime scene."

"Technically, it is. Something was stolen from you," Janet pointed out.

"We'd rather be safe than sorry," Debbie said, easing the moment. "It's curious that they came in and didn't touch your laptop or anything pricey in the doll area, even though some of your antique dolls are worth hundreds. Just the rag doll."

"I hadn't thought of that," Sadie said.

"So why is that?" she continued. "The doll seems to have sparked something. Either nostalgia or old-fashioned theft."

"It must be nostalgia," Estelle said. "There's no real value in an old rag doll. Nothing that would make someone sneak in and steal it." She patted Sadie's shoulder in sympathy. "And you with enough to do around here already." Estelle swept a long look over the kitchen and the front room. "My, what a difference you've made. I'd hardly know the place."

"Clearing the shop out has been a big task, but a loving one." Sadie hesitated, as if she wanted to say more, but then thought better of it. She brought a pitcher of iced tea and four glasses to the table.

Janet set a box of cookies on the table as Debbie and Estelle took seats. "Maybe it was taken for sentimental value," she suggested as she lifted the cover on the white bakery box. "Do you have family that might want the doll, Sadie?"

"Not that I know of. And wouldn't they simply ask me for it?"

"People can get crazy about inheritances." Estelle took a sip of her tea and sat back. "I've seen enough funerals to know that the deceased's decisions can set family members at each other's throats."

Debbie helped herself to a cookie. "My mother says the same thing. She says weddings and funerals can bring out the best and worst in people."

"Maybe Ian can get prints off the key," Janet said. "It's a long shot, but worth asking him about. Estelle, you worked with Lena?"

"For years," she said. "We were both baby boomers, so we had plenty to talk about. I worked in publishing, and she worked here, but we had a lot more time to work together after I retired. Both single, never married. We had a lot in common, you see. Except for our ages," she pointed out in a firmer tone. "You wouldn't think a gap of three years would make a big difference, but it did in some ways. She was more old-school, I was more modern, and yet we were still the best of friends. I was devastated when she passed away."

Janet couldn't imagine.

Sadness tugged at the laugh lines framing Estelle's blue eyes. "It was like a door closed that I can never reopen. Death is like that." She took another sip of her tea.

"I know." Debbie sent her a look of compassion. "And somehow we move on."

"Because we must," Estelle replied. The bright note was back in her voice. "I don't mean to rush you all, but I have to get home in time for a marathon of my favorite TV show on cable. Sadie, did you find any other vintage wonders in the attic?"

"No. Aunt Lena kept piles of this and that for decades. You know her motto. 'Use it up. Wear it out. Make it do or do without.' It's a good way to live, but she took it to extremes."

Janet swallowed a bite of her cookie. "Would you say she was a hoarder?"

"I wouldn't go that far," Sadie said. "But there were definitely a few fire hazards in the house. Going through everything took forever. Some of it I could use or donate, but a lot of it was junk." She grimaced. "If I made a suggestion or offered to help straighten things up when she was alive, she accused me of being pushy. It took a while for me to realize that it meant a lot to her to bring the old and broken back to life, and she wanted to do that wherever she could."

"How in the world did you decide what to keep and what to throw away?" Debbie asked.

"It wasn't easy," Sadie confessed. "Still, I'm happy with the results. I wouldn't have found the rag doll if I hadn't kept plugging away at it. It was a huge relief when they finally picked up the dumpster. I felt like I'd emerged victorious when they carted that away."

"Some of our greatest finds come from odd nooks and crannies." Estelle's lyrical tone reminded Janet of her paternal grandmother, who had spoken with that roller coaster of ups and downs too. Janet missed hearing her voice. "Nothing stays the same forever. Life goes on."

Her words seemed to comfort Sadie, whose expression softened. "Estelle, when you called the other day, you said that Aunt Lena was 'the product of jewels.' That's such a poetic remark. Can you tell us what you meant by it?"

Estelle lifted her brows, and her eyes sparkled. "Gladly. Her mother was a Proverbs 31 woman. Worth more than rubies. Every story I heard about Annie Harper was one of kindness, goodness, and quiet giving. Helping others all the time without drawing attention to herself. If someone needed eggs, Annie had some. If someone needed help weeding their garden, Annie would gather her kids and hurry over to help. Lena said there were times when she hated it because all anyone had to do was call and they'd jump in to help. As she got older, she realized her mother was teaching them that giving is far better than receiving."

Sadie gave a sad smile. "That's funny. I've never heard these stories. Ever."

Estelle waved that off. "You were busy. A young woman with her own sewing business and kids and a doctor husband you helped put through school. There's hardly time to sit and reminisce with all that going on." She finished her tea and stood. "I must get back. It was lovely meeting you, Janet and Debbie. And you, my dear." She aimed a smile at Sadie. "Keep up the good work. Heaven knows you and this place are becoming quite the talk of the town. How wonderful."

Sadie smiled back at her. "Thank you, Estelle. It was good of you to come over. You've made a big difference here over the years."

"It was my pleasure." She tugged her jacket into place and pulled the hood up to thwart the rising wind. "Good night."

As she left, something about her compliments to Sadie bothered Janet. Despite the singsong notes, the words had felt flat. Maybe from something as simple as her dear friend being no longer in the picture.

Or perhaps there was another reason Estelle was less than pleased with Sadie's work on the shop.

CHAPTER ELEVEN

*J*anet turned to Sadie when Estelle had gone. "A key under a rock? That Lena told people about? Anyone who knew that could have come in here, and there's no neighbor on this side of the house between December and April to see them." The couple who lived next door were snowbirds. They went south after the holidays and returned to welcome spring. "It's quite possible that someone knew of that key and let themselves in to get the doll."

"But why?"

Janet frowned. "Maybe they knew about the brooch? Sentimental value? History lover? I don't know."

"Martin Janek seemed pretty angry about me and my entire family," Sadie reminded them. "Do you think he'd come in here and steal the doll?"

"We can't strike him from the list," Janet replied. "But he never mentioned the doll in his tirade."

"And if your aunt Lena knew about him, would she have told him about a spare key?" Debbie asked. "That seems unlikely, given his obvious feelings about your family."

"It does," Sadie agreed. "I can see her sharing that information with neighbors, though. She wasn't one to worry about security because she didn't think anything was worth stealing. Before today, I would have agreed with her. Who'd want a bunch of old broken dolls?" She shrugged. "She probably told a few of the women who helped her sew on and off over the years, and maybe even some doll lovers she knew. People would drop things off for her from time to time when she wasn't home."

"How long has the key been out there?" Debbie asked.

"Your guess is as good as mine. I didn't even know it was there until Estelle mentioned it just now." Sadie shifted her gaze toward the front of the house, thoughtful. "I imagine as long as the rock has been there. Aunt Lena had a regular group of friends years ago that used to meet every couple of weeks, but a lot of them moved south after they retired. One of them painted that rock for her, and it's been in that exact spot in the garden for over twenty-five years. It's never been moved. Always halfway between the dwarf hydrangeas and those pretty yellow and purple crocuses blooming now."

"Lots of people have a favorite hide-a-key spot," Janet said.

"I suppose," Sadie said. "I wish I'd known about Aunt Lena's." She shook herself as if to shake off the gloom then asked, "Have you learned anything?"

"Not much," Janet confessed. "Ruth Franklin mentioned something interesting the other day about your grandmother Mary. It seems she ran into Mary back in the early seventies, over at the county office building. Apparently, Mary was very upset, and Ruth comforted her."

"Poor Grandma," Sadie murmured. "Did she say what was wrong?"

"Apparently she'd come to the county clerk to try to find her birth records. She'd already written to the proper authorities in

Ireland—she said that's where she was born—and learned that the church that held the records had suffered a fire. The county office in New Philadelphia had records of Michael and Lena but nothing on Mary Harper. Ruth said your grandmother told her, 'I guess I'll never know the truth.'"

"Truth about what?" Sadie asked.

"I don't know," Janet admitted. "Perhaps Mary didn't know your family's secrets either."

"I can't even begin to imagine," Sadie said. "What could she possibly mean? And why couldn't the church in Ireland help her? That doesn't make sense."

"Paper records," Debbie reminded her. "They would have been destroyed in the fire."

Sadie sighed. "She was the only one of the children to be born in Ireland. There was a twelve-year gap between her and Aunt Lena. Then two years between Aunt Lena and my great-uncle Michael."

"Twelve years is a long time between children," Debbie mused. "I wonder what caused it."

"My grandmother would have been five when the war started in 1939," Sadie pointed out. "Maybe my great-grandparents put off having more children until things got better."

Sadie picked up her phone and called Estelle. "Sorry to interrupt your marathon, Estelle, but do you know why there was such a big age gap between Aunt Lena and my grandmother?"

"War, I suppose." Estelle's tone sounded reflective, different than when she'd been at the doll hospital mere minutes before. "Threats of war and unrest likely changed things for a lot of people. She told me her parents sent Mary here to the States when she was little, about four or five years old. She lived with her aunt Nessie, Annie's older sister, someplace up in New York. Annie would send blankets and things she'd made from time to time. Like many others, they sent their child where she'd be safe."

"When did they reunite?" Janet asked.

"Annie and Joe came over after the war ended," Estelle said. "I don't know exactly when, but soon after. By then Mary had to be ten or eleven. History tells us that a lot of families back then immigrated by sending a family member or two at a time. War probably made that even more likely."

It was clear that Estelle's answer surprised Sadie. She sat back in her chair, dumbfounded. "She lived here for years without her parents? How have I never heard about this?"

"Hard times get left on the back burner," Estelle replied. "A lot of elderly people don't like to talk about the tough decisions they had to make years ago. Lena said the war was never mentioned in her family. She said anytime she asked about it, her parents either changed the subject or told her they were too busy to answer questions."

"Both my great-uncles acted like they'd taken a vow of silence when anyone mentioned storming the beaches or various battles," Debbie said. "It took a long time for them to be able to talk about it at all. But once they did, it was like a dam opened. They'd head down to McCluskey Park when the weather was nice and talk to other World War II vets. Now my uncles are both gone, and there aren't many of those vets left anymore."

She was right, Janet realized. The Greatest Generation was shrinking fast. She was about to ask a question when a familiar television show jingle came through the phone.

Sadie brought the call to an end. "I'll let you go, Estelle. Sounds like your show is starting."

"It is." Estelle's voice perked up. "Nice chatting with you, as always. Let me know if there's anything else I can help you with."

Sadie ended the call and stared at the phone in her hand. "I had no idea about Mary," she told Debbie and Janet. "I suppose it makes sense, but no one ever even hinted at anything like that."

"What a sacrifice," Janet said. "To send your child to another country for safety while you stay back, caring for the farm in the middle of a war. I don't know that I could have done it. I had a tough enough time letting Tiffany go off to college. Why do you think Annie and Joe stayed behind?"

"No immigration papers?" Sadie shrugged. "Maybe immigration slowed down during the war. I really don't know. My father told me once that by the time the war was over, there wasn't much left of the farm to sell. No one ever explained how that happened in a country that had declared neutrality."

"Neutral doesn't mean no one messed with them," Debbie reminded them. "I'm sure there was some trouble, maybe because they didn't support England outright. I expect not everyone was happy about that."

"The farm had been in my great-grandmother's family for generations." Sadie's expression became wistful. "I'd like to get to Ireland some day and see it for myself, but it's probably a strip mall or something by now."

"Things change," Debbie said. "But that's an interesting turn of events, isn't it? To know that Mary came here before her parents, and years later she tried to find her roots and came up empty."

Janet brought the conversation back around to an earlier idea. "You don't suppose—" She stopped, not wanting to make the suggestion she'd thought of.

Sadie and Debbie watched her, waiting. "Suppose what?" Debbie prompted.

Janet blurted it out. "I was wondering if it was possible that Mary was sent over because she was born out of wedlock. And maybe it was a secret that Annie and Joe didn't want discovered? I'm only suggesting it because public perceptions were quite different then, particularly in Ireland. They might have sent her over to avoid censure."

"So even if she'd found a record of her birth, it might not have been accurate," Janet said. "And it could explain, Sadie, why your father told you to stop asking questions about your heritage. Then again, it might be something else altogether. Ruth Franklin suggested the possibility that Mary thought she was adopted. She also talked about how pale and blond Mary was."

"Like ivory," Sadie said.

"And Lena wasn't like that, was she?"

"No, though I'd never thought about it before. She and Michael were both light-skinned, but they took after Grandpa Joe's family. At least that's what everyone said. Light hair when they were young that turned darker when they were adolescents. But Mary's hair stayed platinum blond, and she was really pale."

"Not all siblings look alike," Debbie reminded them.

"I wish my father was still around," Sadie said. "I called my mother last night, but she was no help at all. Now that Aunt Lena's gone, there's no one to ask."

"Paulette suggested that we talk to Violet Lincoln," Janet said.

"That's right," Debbie said. "I'll call her tonight and ask her if we can get together soon."

After a moment of silence, Janet said, "You know, there is still one more person we could talk to."

"Martin Janek." Debbie must have followed Janet's train of thought.

Sadie stared at them in disbelief for a moment and then sighed. "You're right, of course. Maybe if I can get him to talk calmly, I'll get some answers. It can't hurt to try, right?" She bit her lip. "But what if he won't talk to me?" She gazed pleadingly at Janet and then Debbie. "You'll come, won't you? I don't want to meet with him alone."

"Of course," Janet assured her. "I tell you what. I'll give him a call and see if I can set it up. The worst he can do is say no."

From the Diary of Anya Oleski

Poland
September 1941

I have sent a much-loved child on her way. Doing so touches so many memories, good and bad. And sad.

She seems well. Taller. Her hair is longer, and she's still thin, but that is the case for so many at present.

What a pleasure to have time with this blessed child, although our time must be brief. She is safer in school. We know this. We are willing to sacrifice much to keep her there.

We may see her again come winter. Much will depend on the weather. She has gotten a few letters we have sent, but very few. Such is the way of wartime post.

Nessie has sent me word that all is well there for now, but there is much rumbling on that continent about inaction. I sense her aggravation. It is understandable, because she has family here. A lot of family. And yet, what a hard decision to send your men and even women to battle on the other side of the world. I don't know the right of it, nor the wrong, but I know that help is needed.

I am too sensitive on the days I bid her farewell. It brings too much to mind. Not knowing when I will see her again. If I will see her again. Not knowing how she will fare.

My fingers quiver and my palms sweat, and yet my Joseph goes off with a child in tow and faces the world with a calm I envy.

I sew a lot these days. Anything to keep my hands and mind busy. In that way I will be ready when I see her again. I can teach her the ways of the needle, a skill passed on. Some call it art.

It is a fanciful assertion from a luxurious era I despair of ever seeing again, although it certainly can be artful.

It is a basic skill to take care of oneself, to provide for oneself, to know how to sew, with or without a machine. Power is in short supply, but the treadle needs no power other than mine and, oddly enough, my heart settles in as I piece things together.

That is enough for now.

Kielce, Poland
December 1941

Oh, Nessie. I hate to write this, and yet I must.

It is with deepest sorrow that I report our beloved Frank has gone home to God.

I have no details. I don't know when, really, or where. Simply that he's gone and with us no more.

Part of me yearns to know more, but another part sits in stunned silence.

Our cousin was a dear man and a good friend to so many. He will be greatly missed here. Our Frank was not a man slated for battle, but when the need arose, I am certain he did the best he could. He had no choice, of course. Few do, now. So many were sent to the far north on the opposite side of the river, and yet Germany has taken that now too, so no one knows what is to become of anyone or anything. In my heart I plan for days to come. In my head I deal with the here and now, with so many unsaid farewells.

Frank loved us. All of us. We are blessed to have known him and loved him in return. I wish our time had not been cut short. As always, I wish for peace to reign, but in the midst of turmoil, I take solace in putting things together. Another example of that is en route to you and George, but as I write this I hear of a change in your status, what with America entering the war.

Will George even be there? What will happen if he is not?

And yet, dearest sister, I know God reigns. I know He loves us and watches over us and has put into our hands a means to share with one another, even if nothing more than simple scraps of leftover fabric. Putting those to good use isn't just a skill now. It is a time of tranquility in a stormy sea, and it brings me peace. I know that my Redeemer lives and has welcomed dear Frank into His precious domain.

Joseph conducts his routes as always, stalwart and strong. Food is scarce in many places, but he squirrels away half a sandwich here and a potato there. He cannot be obvious, so he slips things to me quietly. "Enough," I tell him, for I cannot bear the thought of him getting caught and the horrific consequences that will follow.

He laughs and takes my hands into his. "No one will begrudge a hard worker the chance to keep a bite for later. If ever they don't need me, it could be

different, my love, but they do need me and the few oth-
ers who understand the workings of this engine. The
engine keeps me safe. The dresses keep you safe.
Perhaps it was for this very thing that God pre-
pared us."

His words bolster me.

He practices English when he is home. He didn't
bother much with it before the invasion, thinking
we'd grow old here, but now he practices with me,
learning to pronounce things the English way. He
tells me that when he cannot practice out loud, he
practices in his mind, and he is truly improving. You
and I learned so young that it became second nature
to us. So perhaps all those things leading up to now
were to help us survive and, in turn, help others. How
it must break God's heart to see evil among His peo-
ple, and yet it has been that way from our beginnings
in the Garden of Eden.

Dear Joseph is an honorable man in his efforts.
His dependability and knowledge of steam engines
has kept him here, serving the constant movement
of people and officers. A man of valor is surely a bless-
ing. The news earlier this month might change our
ability to communicate, but I will send prayers and
love and bits of this and that as I am able.

May God bless each of us and our families.

I weep at the loneliness of it all, but then I dry my tears and do what I can for others because that is what Baba taught us. And she was a woman of great wisdom. I love you, Nessie. Please share that love with your wonderful family.

Ever your sister,

Anya

CHAPTER TWELVE

Janet and Debbie headed home. Debbie drove while Janet looked up Martin's number.

She called him, but there was no answer.

She left a quick message then followed it up with a text. My name is Janet Shaw. Sadie Flaherty, Debbie Albright, and I would like to chat with you about your visit to That's My Baby, the doll hospital. We don't know why you are so upset and would like to talk to you to see if we can work things out. Please call or text me if you are willing to meet with us.

She didn't have to wait long.

A text came through within a couple of minutes. Thursday is good.

Three thirty? texted Janet.

Yes. At the doll place?

Sounds good.

He sent a thumbs-up emoji.

Janet was about to slide her phone back into her pocket when another text chimed in, this one from Kim. Good Shepherd is allowing visitors as of tomorrow! You can call Mom and set things up whenever.

She read the text to Debbie, and Debbie sent her a questioning glance as she pulled up to a stop sign. "You've got Tiffany's birthday coming up, and we've got Doughnut Days this weekend. I don't want to make you or your baking schedule crazy. Should we postpone going to Good Shepherd until after the weekend?"

Janet shrugged. "I'm fine. And with your dad and mine manning the fryers for Doughnut Days, all I have to do is mix the glaze and make the dough. They take it from there. I say let's do it in case they have to quarantine again?"

Debbie steered into Janet's driveway. "Good point. Okay, I'll see you in the morning. Hey, what's that?" she asked as she put the car in park.

Another slip of paper flapped beneath the wiper on Janet's windshield. They both climbed out and approached the car. Janet lifted the paper by the edge and let it open in the breeze. "'Business people should always think twice about what they're doing and maybe what they've done. You might want to back away and leave things alone.'"

Debbie shook her finger at the note. "If anyone thinks a stupid warning like that is going to deter us, they've got another think coming. They don't scare us."

Janet folded the note. "But who is leaving the notes? And why? And is this because we're helping Sadie, or because of something else we've done since we opened the café?"

"The timing points to Sadie's situation, but we have managed to ruffle a few feathers over the past nine months." Debbie was fuming now, which was rare. "As to the why, I have no idea, but something like this actually makes me more determined to figure things out."

"Agreed," Janet said. "I'll call Eileen right now and see if we can set something up for tomorrow after work. And I'll check with the neighbors to see if anyone noticed anything or caught anything on their cameras."

"Good." Debbie gave her a quick hug. "I'll call Violet. Let me know if you find out anything, okay?"

"I will."

Eileen was over the moon at the prospect of company, but Janet struck out with the neighbors. Only one of their cameras caught Janet's house, and that was from the wrong angle. No one had anything to show who'd slipped the paper beneath her windshield wiper.

Ian had called earlier that day and said he'd be working late. When he finally got home, he scowled at the note. "They came to our house in broad daylight to warn you? And nobody caught anything on their cameras?"

"They came while I was at Sadie's with Debbie," she said. "Did Evan's wife have the baby?"

He nodded, but the happy news didn't ease his expression. "Yes, and Mom and baby are both doing well. A boy, a little over seven pounds and not too wrinkled."

Janet laughed. "I remember how worried you were that something was wrong with Tiffany because of how odd she looked as a newborn."

He acknowledged that with a slight wince. "In my defense, I was unschooled in the ways of infants, newborns, diapers, and anything to do with onesies. I learned, though."

"And you're a wonderful dad," she told him.

He pulled her close, but he was still frowning. "I don't like this," he said gruffly. "I don't like that someone feels comfortable doing this in the middle of the day to intimidate the wife of the chief of police."

"I don't either, but honestly, what can this person do? Nothing," she told him firmly. "The café has passed all the first tests. The first month, first autumn, the first holiday season, and now we've gotten through the first winter. That's always the test for a new business, when the weather turns and no one wants to go out. I think this person is trying to scare us off. But we did get the camera outside the café fixed, so if they do it again in the parking lot, we can see them."

"I should have checked those cameras," he grumbled. "Kim said the feed was strange, and I didn't take the time to check it. What if something had happened to you?"

"I'd get a well-deserved day off," she joked. When he glared at her, she nudged him playfully. "It's a silly note, Ian."

"Of a somewhat threatening nature, aimed at my wife."

"Trying to scare us. Perhaps trying to keep us from helping a friend discover the truth about this doll and her family. It can't possibly be all that nefarious if all they're doing is leaving anonymous notes, Ian." She thought of something that would cheer him up. "I bought steak yesterday."

His mood lightened instantly. "We haven't had that in a long time."

"And that's why I bought it." She grabbed an apron from a wall hook and tied it on. "If you light the grill, I'll get potatoes going."

"And you'll be careful?"

"With the potatoes?" She winked at him. "Super careful."

He leaned down and kissed her. "I just want you safe, love. You and Tiffany are everything to me."

He wasn't an overly sentimental type, so she reached up and cupped his face in both hands. "I will be careful. Always. And thank you for watching out for me."

"Well, you do make the best potato casserole around." He smiled to show he'd let the topic drop. That was another thing she loved about him. He never went off the deep end. That quality and his fair-minded, common-sense nature held him in good stead as police chief.

But he'd made a good point.

It was bold of the note writer to come into their neighborhood and leave a note in full view of anyone. Whoever it was had been lucky not to be seen.

Lucky?

Smart?

Or both?

She wasn't sure, but she was determined to find out.

From the Diary of Anya Oleski

Poland
January 1942

America has entered the war.

Joseph has said so.

News doesn't reach this corner of the nation readily, but as he guides the train, he is privy to information others don't or cannot know. He keeps these things to himself, never speaking of anything controversial.

We work for these people so that we may live.

We despise the choice.

We pray for the Lord's forgiveness.

And we pray for our precious girl and all the other children of oppression.

CHAPTER THIRTEEN

Janet texted Debbie before she went to bed that night. WE CAN MEET WITH EILEEN AND RAY AROUND THREE TOMORROW. SOUND GOOD?

Yes, Debbie texted back. I PROMISED MOM I'D HELP HER PUT UP SOME WINDOW BOXES, BUT WE'LL HAVE PLENTY OF TIME TO DO THAT AFTER SUPPER. I LOVE DAYLIGHT SAVING TIME. She added three smiling sunny emojis to make her point.

Janet responded, ME TOO. AFTER A WEEK OR SO.

Debbie responded with a laughing emoji then added, I CALLED VIOLET. SHE SAYS SHE'LL COME TO THE CAFÉ TOMORROW AROUND TWO THIRTY. PAULETTE WILL BE THERE, SO IT WON'T TAKE LONG TO CLOSE, AND WE SHOULD HAVE TIME.

SOUNDS GOOD, Janet replied. SEE YOU IN THE MORNING!

Morning felt mighty early the next day.

Janet hated the initial effects of moving the clock forward. The lost hour took some getting used to through the first week, but the extra hour of daylight in the evening made the sacrifice well worth it.

The café was in roller-coaster mode all morning.

Busy, quiet, busy, quiet, then busy again. Not unusual, but choppy enough that Janet felt like she couldn't quite catch up with what she needed to get done before a hectic weekend, despite her early start.

Greg strolled into the café around one thirty, when the lunch rush was over and all that was left were a few stragglers. Sawdust lightened the knees of his blue jeans. His nicked knuckles testified to his industry with her neighbor's bathroom.

Janet smiled his way, but he didn't notice her. He was too busy looking over her shoulder, his face lit up. Janet followed his gaze. To her complete lack of surprise, Debbie stood there, grinning back at him.

He approached the counter. "Sorry I'm a mess. I fought with an old bit of plumbing for over an hour, and the pipe was determined to emerge triumphant."

He took a seat at the counter, and Debbie poured coffee into a mug. "Who won?" she asked him.

He grinned and flexed his right arm. "Perseverance and a stubborn nature, naturally."

She chuckled and set the mug in front of him.

"Thank you," he told her, picking it up and taking a gulp. "The weather is brutal again today. Is it too late to get a hot roast beef with Swiss on a toasted roll?"

"Not at all." They exchanged smiles, and Janet started toward the kitchen to make his sandwich. She stopped when she heard Debbie say, "You're working next door to Janet's house, right?"

"Kind of," he told her. "It's technically two doors down, but it's a weird configuration, because the house between is set back from the street. One of the old places from before they blacktopped roads and made zoning rules."

"Someone left a note on Janet's car yesterday," Debbie told him. "Did you happen to notice anyone out and about? Or near her place?"

He shook his head. "A couple of dog walkers through the day, but I wasn't exactly watching out the window. We were doing demo, so it was a mess. I heard the school bus let kids off up the road, but other than that, it was quiet. No one around that I saw. This wet weather keeps people in almost as much as the winter cold does. A few cars headed toward the park, and a couple went up the other end of the street, around the bend. I heard them slow down, but I wasn't really paying attention."

Frustrated, Janet went to the kitchen to make Greg's sandwich.

When she set it in front of him a few minutes later, he asked, "What did this note say?"

Janet spoke softly as Debbie refilled his coffee. "It told us to back off and leave things alone."

"And all this is because you're investigating an old doll? Or do you think it's something else?" He jutted his chin toward Debbie as she wiped the counter. "Debbie filled me in on what you guys were doing."

Debbie filled him in...

Janet tucked that nugget of girlfriend-style information away for later teasing. "It means we hit a nerve somewhere. We just don't know where."

"Nothing came up on the camera feeds?" Greg frowned.

"No. The cameras don't reach that side of the garage."

"So anyone could have pulled up, dropped off the note, and gone on their way."

She nodded. "And if they backed up, they'd never pass the camera Ian has on the front of the house."

"That's frustrating," Greg said. "I'll keep my ears open and watch that way when I hear someone slow down. But I'm having a hard time believing anyone around here would be upset with you and Debbie investigating an old doll."

Janet wasn't sure whether Debbie had told Greg about the brooch, but it seemed like she hadn't. His skepticism was understandable. Fussing over a musty rag doll didn't make much sense on the surface.

Fussing about a beautiful vintage emerald brooch was a whole other conversation.

They were almost done with cleanup when Violet Lincoln knocked on the glass of the café door.

Janet hurried over and unlocked the door. "Violet, thank you so much for coming," she said as the woman bustled in. "Would you like a cup of coffee and a cinnamon roll while we visit?"

"I would never refuse a Janet Shaw cinnamon roll," Violet said with a chuckle. "And if you happen to have one with extra icing, that would be even better."

Debbie poured three cups of coffee and plated a couple of cinnamon rolls—one with extra icing. She grabbed one more plate and some silverware, then carried everything on a tray to the table where Janet and Violet were discussing the ladies guild's current projects.

Paulette emerged from the kitchen, pulling on her gloves. "I need to get going, but I think we're all done. I'll see you ladies in the morning." She smiled at Violet. "And I'll see you at the meeting on Friday," she said. "I hope we're going to discuss what to do with the money Tildy Jackson donated to the guild. I have some ideas."

"It's on the agenda," Violet assured her. "I'm expecting that will take up most of our time." She grinned. "We are nothing if not opinionated."

Paulette waved and went out the door. Debbie put a cinnamon roll in front of Violet, cut the other one in half, and gave one of the halves to Janet on the extra plate. "You good with this?" she asked her.

"More than good," Janet said. "You read my mind."

Violet took a bite of her roll then washed it down with a sip of coffee. "Every bit as delicious as I remembered. Now, what can I help you with?"

"Mary Harper," Janet said. "Paulette told us that you visited her when she was sick."

"I did," Violet said. "That was a few years ago now—about six or seven, I think."

"We were wondering if there is anything you could tell us about her past," Debbie said. "Did she talk about her parents, or the war, or coming to the States when she was little?"

Janet noticed that Debbie didn't mention that Mary had spent the war years apart from her parents. She caught Debbie's eye and gave a very slight nod. That was best for now.

"Not that I recall. She wasn't very responsive by the time I was seeing her." Violet took another bite of her roll and chewed thoughtfully. "But there was something strange, now that I think about it. "There were a few times when she would murmur things under her breath, and once or twice when she called out."

"But that's not strange, is it?" Debbie asked, her expression quizzical. "I mean, don't a lot of people do that when they're not fully conscious or when they're sleeping?"

"It wasn't the fact that she did those things that was strange," said Violet. "It was the language she spoke in. I'm not sure what it was, but I can assure you it was not Irish."

They pulled into the parking lot of Good Shepherd right around three. Janet was looking forward to seeing both their elderly friends, especially Ray. When she'd been there to visit Eileen the last couple of times, Ray had been out doing one thing or another, so it had been a while. Ray Zink had served in World War II and then came home and worked for the county land management services, taking care of parks and gardens for decades. He had never married, but he and Eileen had developed a solid friendship over the years, and his eyes always held an extra spark whenever she entered a room.

Debbie and Janet signed in and found Ray and Eileen in the solarium. "Out of captivity, are we?" Janet joked when she saw them.

"Finally!" Eileen declared. "Being stuck in one's room for a week is akin to prison. Remind me not to break any major laws."

Ray was more easygoing. "They do what they have to do, of course," he told Janet as she and Debbie sat down. "Otherwise, you've got family upset that their loved ones aren't being taken care of. And no one wants anyone to get sick. Especially at our age."

"It's good that they err on the side of caution," Eileen agreed begrudgingly. "I appreciate it. I really do. But that doesn't make it any easier, that's for sure."

"It's March, so we might be at the end of it," Ray said hopefully. "That kind of thing doesn't much happen in the spring and summer. Winter, mostly."

"You gals were coming over to check something out, right?" Eileen folded her hands primly, a sweet gesture left over from a different time.

"We're looking into a few things for Sadie Flaherty," Debbie explained.

"Her aunt, Lena Harper, ran the doll hospital over in Uhrichsville," Janet reminded her.

"I knew the Harpers back in the day," Ray said. "They were our neighbors up the road, an older couple. Joe and—" He struggled for a moment, searching for a name.

"Annie?" Janet prompted.

He pointed a finger at her. "That's it, yes. Annie. Nice family. Neat as a pin. We shared garden vegetables with each other from time to time. A lot of tomatoes." His eyes took on a faraway look. "And squash, always squash. That Annie made the best bread out of the green squash."

Janet smiled. "Zucchini bread?"

Ray smiled too. "Yes, that's what she called it. A couple slices of that smeared with real butter, and a fellow could work half the day. It was that hearty."

"Did you know their daughter Mary?" Debbie asked.

He considered. "She was the oldest one. I remember a group of boys used to call her 'Pale Mary,' making fun of her light hair and skin. I heard them doing it one time, and I went over the back fence and put a stop to it right then. There's no call for being mean."

"She was very fair-skinned," Eileen added. "And quiet. Not shy, necessarily. Just not exuberant the way so many children are. Annie worried that sending her over to the States by herself might have been hard on the girl."

"Estelle Parkin told us about that," Janet said. "Lena told her. Lena said her mother would never talk about it."

"I didn't hear it from Annie. I heard it from Joe." Eileen sipped water through a straw from a cup nearby. "Joe Harper was a train-man from the get-go. He knew trains, he understood routes, and he kept a sharp eye on the weather. He could tell what an engine needed from the sound of it, and he was always listening. He always said the engines spoke to him and told him what they needed. He was invaluable to the Pennsylvania Railroad, let me tell you."

"That's impressive," Debbie remarked.

She took another sip. "Joe wasn't much of a talker," she said after she swallowed. "But one day we grabbed a sandwich together in the back room, and he saw a picture of my family when I was digging in my purse for a napkin. That was when I was subbing for someone who was out with back problems. It was a long recovery time, and the kids were in school full-time, so I was happy to do it. Anyway, we were in that little break area together. He smiled at the picture of me, Rafe, and the kids and said, 'You are blessed, Eileen Palmer. Me too.'"

"How sweet," Debbie murmured.

"I remember it because for a moment his voice changed," Eileen said. "I asked him, 'How's that, Joe? The blessing?'"

"He said, 'To have family here, all safe.'" Eileen's voice grew softer, and Janet leaned in to hear her. "And then he went on to say his wife worried about Mary. They were afraid that sending her over here before everyone else was a mistake and that she might feel unloved, even if it was for her own good."

Janet hadn't considered how such a small girl must have felt about being sent away from her home, from her family. How could a five-year-old understand that she was being protected when it must have felt like rejection?

Eileen's expression became thoughtful. "He seemed alarmed after he said that, almost frightened. But before I could ask him about it, he grabbed his sandwich and headed out the door. It wasn't so much his words that put that scene so firm in my memory, but his actions. They were so different from his usual self. And his expression, that glimpse of fear, set me to wondering, but war's like that. Folks make hard choices they'd never make in normal times. But there's nothing normal about war."

"Too true," Ray said.

"Folks romanticize it now, so far removed from the reality of it. But there's nothing romantic about the darkness that comes from war. It is horrible in extremes for so many people." Eileen gazed at them, her eyes bright. "I think that's why what we did here in Dennison was so special. Making sure folks came out to welcome the troops, bring them food, coffee, doughnuts, hot chocolate, cider. Little things to show them we appreciated their efforts. Let them know they were cared for. Even if they had no family to send them off, they had us, and it helped more than a few, let me tell you."

To lighten the atmosphere, Janet tugged a small box of scones that Eileen loved from her tote bag. "Glazed almond scones," she announced. "Enough to share."

Eileen and Ray both smiled with excitement.

As Janet passed around the scones, she asked, "Eileen, when you say Joe's voice changed, do you mean his tone? Going from happy to regret or worry?"

"No." Eileen broke off a small piece of her scone and popped it into her mouth. "It was like a different person talking altogether. Then I never heard it again. Joe was a soft-spoken man. Even his accent was soft."

"He was from Ireland," Debbie reminded them.

Eileen shook her head. "I didn't hear much Irish in it. I'm not perfect at identifying accents, but his sounded very different."

"Annie had more of an Irish sound than Joe did," Ray said. "English too. I thought she was from England at first, the way she talked, but she explained that they were from Ireland. I guess they talk different from place to place, like we do here. You know, Boston natives don't sound like those from Georgia, and Georgia people don't sound like Louisiana residents, and so forth. For a long time, we sounded more Midwest around these parts, but we've got more drawl than we used to."

"Definitely more drawl than you used to find in eastern Ohio," Eileen agreed. "But that's the way of things, isn't it? Guaranteed to change."

Janet covered Eileen's hand with one of her own. "It sure is."

Ray yawned, then made a face. Even at nearly ninety-nine years of age and wheelchair-bound, Ray Zink made it a point to enjoy every day of his life. He'd once confided to Janet that he hated the idea of sleeping it away.

Still, Janet stood. "You've both been a big help. I've got to get home to get supper going, and Debbie's helping her mom tonight, so we'll duck out. Thank you both." She didn't bend to hug them as she usually would have. After all, she worked in a customer-facing job, and while her immune system might fight off anything she picked up from their patrons, she wouldn't risk Ray or Eileen getting sick. A little social distance was a small price to pay when the retirement center had just reopened their doors to the public. "Can we bother you again if we think of anything else?"

"You're never a bother." Eileen's firm tone said she meant it. "And I'll call you if anything else comes to mind. One thing I can say for certain—the Harpers were good people. Salt of the earth. The kind of folks I would have liked to have known better."

"Best seal of approval I've ever heard," Janet told her.

She and Debbie walked out together.

It wasn't windy, and the temperature had risen into the low fifties—almost a heat wave for Ohio in March. Janet paused by her car door and recapped what they'd heard inside. "Salt of the earth. Honest. Hardworking. We didn't get much new information, did we?"

"No." Debbie shrugged. "But we got confirmation from reliable sources that the Harpers were good people, though they might not have been from Ireland. And it seems that Annie realized Mary was struggling a bit, longing for roots she couldn't find. But she went on to raise a family and work in Sugarcreek. So she got over it? Or dealt with it and moved on?"

"Could be either," Janet said. "I know I don't appreciate the past like I should. I don't mean being a history buff, because I do like history. The people around here are steeped in history, and it's hard not to gain a respect and affinity for it, but I never dig into my own family history. Their times, their struggles."

"You might do that once you retire and have more time," Debbie suggested.

"Maybe." Janet frowned. "But if we're all too busy to pay attention to the past, how do we lay a solid path to the future?"

"Kindness. Goodness. Great cookies."

Janet laughed.

"I think we're helping to keep the past in people's minds by working in the depot," Debbie said more seriously. "When they come into the café, they're surrounded by history, and the museum is right outside our door. Dennison made history long before the war by being a strategic point on the rails and then continued that for decades after." She checked her watch. "What time do we meet with Martin Janek tomorrow?"

"Three thirty."

"At the doll hospital?"

Janet nodded. "Yes. I would have preferred neutral ground, but he suggested that location, and I didn't want to argue." A timer on her phone went off. She silenced it and beamed. "Tiffany's due to arrive in an hour, and I want to have supper waiting. I figured out last fall that she doesn't necessarily come home to see *us*." She chuckled as she opened the car door. "She comes home to do her laundry and see her friends. And have her own shower for a couple of days. But I'll take what I can get."

"I remember doing that." Debbie acknowledged Janet's comment with a wry expression. "That first year of college was an eye-opener, for certain."

They headed in opposite directions, Debbie to help her mom with the window boxes and Janet to greet her beloved daughter. The goodbyes of having a college girl were still tough, but the welcome homes were absolutely marvelous. While they lasted, of course.

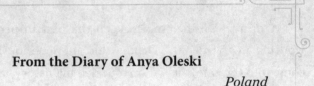

From the Diary of Anya Oleski

Poland
March 1942

It is cold. Deeply cold. Bone-chillingly cold. Bitter temperatures and wind seem to blast right through the walls of the house. A north-facing window was broken in late November. We boarded over the opening and chinked the edges, but a stout wind will pass directly through the wood.

We've sent a new blanket off to a family in need.

Yes, it is cold here, but the blanket will give respite to someone worse off than we are. I am hopeful that my letters and gifts to Nessie have gone through, though nothing has come back. That may mean success, but my sense of security in that could be false. If war has taught me anything good in face of the bad, it is the pleasant surprise that some people risk so much to help. As always, there are those who do not subscribe to evil, even among the German troops. Some turn a blind eye, but it is hard to know if that is truth or an act to build confidence, tricking one into carelessness.

I am a mother. I cannot afford a moment of carelessness. I have no confidence in them. I have no confidence in what used to be reality.

I have confidence only in God, in His deliverance and in His grace, because He would never have people treat each other so. Satan, yes. God, no.

Why is man so inclined to power and greed? Why do people make such choices? Isn't it so much better to fill an emptiness with God, with His Son, with faith?

How much colder is a life without faith?

Coal and wood have been diverted to people of prominence. Snow has slowed or blocked trains many times. Or maybe the supply has grown low. I would not be surprised by that.

News is scarce.

I hate not knowing. I hate being in the dark throes of an everlasting winter. That is an exaggeration, I know, but it is also a sensation caused by lack of direction and knowledge, and more and more cold.

One of my clients has arranged for a coal delivery to me. "How can Anya ply a needle with frozen hands?" she demanded.

I don't know if it will come.

If it does, I shall use it sparingly and with a grateful heart, for it could be the sole delivery this season, and there is no wood to burn.

But it is easy to keep food fresh and frozen right now. That is an unexpected blessing.

CHAPTER FOURTEEN

rue to Janet's prediction, she and Ian got an hour or so with Tiffany before she headed off to meet some high school buddies at a friend's house. But that was all right. They'd raised a grounded daughter who'd made the dean's list her first semester.

The second Tiffany stepped out the door, Janet remembered that she'd meant to ask her daughter about the dresser. That was what phones were for. Before she forgot again, she texted her daughter an explanation, as well as several photos of the piece, so Tiffany could check it out at her leisure.

Ian was caught up in a book, so Janet opened her laptop and typed *Martin Janek* into the search engine.

Several things came up. Nothing of great note. A few locations, his parents' obituaries, and a mention in articles about fundraisers for a church in New Philadelphia.

A text from Sadie interrupted her research. This time it was a group text that included Debbie. ANOTHER ANONYMOUS EMAIL. NOW THEY WANT TO MEET ME. OR RATHER, THEY'RE THREATENING TO MEET ME. FORWARDING IT TO YOU. WHAT SHOULD I DO?

Sadie's concern came through loud and clear.

Janet went into the kitchen and video-called Debbie and Sadie right away. "Sadie, will you read us the email?"

Sadie obliged. "'Dear Sadie,'" she read, "'I've been thinking about our situation. It is, admittedly, difficult. I'm not one to break promises, but I currently see no other choice. I'd like to come that way and meet you. It's time for people to know the truth. I understood the initial silence, the veil of secrecy, but circumstances have changed. I must come, you see. I simply need to arrange transportation down there.' Then it's signed the way the first one was." Sadie held up a printout so that Janet and Debbie could see it. "Two initials. M.E."

Debbie frowned. "'Transportation down there,'" she mused. "So this person is north of us? And I'm guessing by the tone of the email, it's a woman."

"How can you tell that?" Sadie asked.

Debbie shifted her left eyebrow up as she answered. "Well, there's no way to be sure, of course, but the tone seems a little softer than most men write, at least to me. 'I'd like to come that way and meet you,'" she quoted. "Most guys would say something more like, 'Possibly heading your way soon. Would like to meet you. Checking on transportation.'"

"I think you're right," Janet agreed.

"I'd have never thought of that," Sadie said. "But I see it now that you've pointed it out. And I'm less worried about a woman than a man."

"Statistics back you up on that," Janet said. "But it's weird that the person chooses to remain anonymous, yet at the same time expresses the desire to meet you."

"And I don't like the tone." Debbie's mouth quirked in annoyance. "They sound threatening but could easily claim that's not what they meant."

"It's either very cleverly done, or we're reading something into nothing," Janet said. "On another note, I did some research on Martin Janek. I haven't found much except some church work and his parents' obituaries. No mention of any Harpers."

"I hope he's in a better mood when we meet up with him tomorrow," said Sadie. "I never dreamed I'd stir up a hornet's nest by posting an old rag doll online. Who'd have thought?"

Janet shrugged. "Not me, for sure. But sometimes all it takes is a mention of something done wrong or gone wrong, and it hits all the triggers or buttons self-help books talk about. And sometimes the person doesn't even know why. Debbie and I will get there before three, okay, Sadie? That way we're ready when he shows up."

"But don't you have to get ready for the Doughnut Days on Friday and Saturday?"

"Our dads are getting everything set up," Debbie told her. "It's like old times when they helped us with campouts and the sled races we had in school every January. With or without snow."

"All right." Sadie's expression relaxed. "I don't want to be interfering with your business."

Janet didn't mention that she'd be working extra early the next two days to fill orders for Celtic-themed cupcakes and cookies. Sadie had enough on her plate. "We're like a well-oiled machine. No worries."

She saw Debbie hide a smirk, but Sadie accepted her words.

"Good. I don't know how to thank you both for helping me. It means a lot."

"Glad to do it," Debbie declared. "Part of the fun of being home again is reconnecting with old friends. And if there's a puzzle involved, all the better. But I'll be happy when we can all get together, have coffee, or go out for dinner, and just be ourselves. When this is over, okay?"

"I'd love nothing more." Sadie smiled into the camera.

So did Janet. "See you both tomorrow." She disconnected the call and clicked to the page she'd left open.

Martin Janek's name sat in her search bar, with very few links below it. She scanned them once again, and her eye stopped on a link to his involvement with the church.

The reference was a highlighted link to their website. She clicked on it and found an article written by the secretary and published in a small local newspaper in New Philadelphia.

Dead center in that article was a picture of a lovely church with a rich Polish history. A work crew was arranged in the churchyard, and a small, old-time rectory was located to one side. The people in the picture posed with paint cans, brushes, and rollers. Janet skimmed the caption underneath and caught the names Martin Janek, Amalie Janek, and Susan Janek. Amalie and Susan couldn't have been more than ten years old, but they each held a trowel, clearly proud of their efforts.

A glimpse inside the rectory showed the fruits of their labors and touted the volunteer's spirit that had brought folks together to refurbish the old building.

Martin stood to one side behind his two children. He was smiling and had his arms slung around the shoulders of the men on either side of him. It was a very happy group and a drastically different image of the man who'd shown up at That's My Baby in a rage.

Her phone pinged with a text from Tiffany, which made her smile. LOVE THE DRESSER. DO WE HAVE PAINT, MAYBE WHITE AND BLUE? I WANTED TO ASK BEFORE YOU GO TO BED. I WANT TO WORK ON IT TOMORROW.

WE HAVE BOTH IN THE BASEMENT, Janet texted back. PLENTY OF WHITE SATIN BUT ALSO AT LEAST ONE SHADE OF BLUE. FEEL FREE TO MIX AWAY LIKE YOU USED TO DO WITH YOUR MODELING CLAY. She added a laughing emoji because once, when Tiffany was little, she had mixed all her clay together—the red, blue, yellow, orange, and green—only to find that the result was a muddy grayish-green camouflage color. Despite her take-charge nature, Tiffany wasn't a camo kind of girl, so she never did that again.

Tiffany texted a string of laughing emojis. I REMEMBER THAT! LET'S SEE IF MY SKILL WITH COLORS HAS IMPROVED. LOVE YOU.

LOVE YOU TOO, SWEETIE.

Janet laid out her jeans and a shamrock-covered long-sleeve T-shirt for the morning. Greeting the customers in a fun T-shirt was one of her favorite things, and dancing shamrocks for mid-March was absolutely perfect.

And maybe it would bring her a little luck for the meeting with Martin tomorrow.

CHAPTER FIFTEEN

Well-oiled machine, huh?" Janet scowled at the normally dependable double oven that chose to be temperamental at a quarter
to five in the morning.

She had six dozen cupcakes and ten dozen cookies on order, all
to be picked up tomorrow, and she also needed to stock their bakery
case for the day.

She texted Debbie and then her mother, grateful that she had
always been an early riser. Mom, need your oven for cake and
cookie orders. café oven is broken. If I prep everything, can
you bake, fill, and frost cupcakes? And bake cookies? I'll
have the batter and dough ready when you get here.

Her mother texted back minutes later. Preheating oven to
350. On my way with help.

Debbie's mother texted her two minutes later. Riding shotgun
In my pajamas! Cavalry to the rescue!

Debbie had walked in and grinned when Janet showed her
the text. "She spelled it right this time. Ninety percent of the time
she says 'calvary' and spells it the same way, but it makes her mad
that she confuses the two words. Mom doesn't like to make
mistakes."

"The apple didn't fall far from the tree," Janet told her.

Debbie pulled on one of the train-decorated aprons. "Admittedly. I am known for my obsession with being informed and always knowing what I'm doing. Which makes getting swoony over a guy with two teenagers fairly frightening. I don't know much about kids, I don't have any brothers, and my experience in that arena is nil, so what do I think I'm doing?" Her frown said she wasn't necessarily hoping for answers but that the question was important.

"You're taking a chance." Janet kept it simple. "Exploring your options. Exactly what we're doing here." She swept the café with a quick glance. "And in our personal lives. We're at a new stage, and I think that's okay."

"Except for the broken oven."

Janet groaned as she dropped two sticks of butter into a large mixing bowl. "I texted Allie's Appliance, and she said she'll make us a priority. But she went on to say that getting the right parts might take a couple of days. Fortunately, I have stock in the freezer. Baked crusts, a few layer cakes, and several dozen cookies and muffins." Freezing some things ahead of time was a lesson she'd learned at the Third Street Bakery, where she'd honed her skills in commercial baking. "With so much focus on Doughnut Days this weekend, I should be able to skate by with our mothers' combined efforts. And here they are."

Mom and Becca came in the back door together.

In minutes they'd packed the car with trays, shamrock-themed wrappers, baking pans, parchment paper, two batches of dark chocolate cupcake batter, and three batches of cookie dough, ready to scoop.

"I'm doing cookies at my place," Becca announced. "I'm not the baker Lorilee is, but I can manage those, since you've got the dough already made."

"Batter up!" Mom laughed and mimicked a baseball batter's stance. "I'll do cupcakes, and we'll pick up frostings and fillings in a couple of hours, okay? These orders are all for tomorrow, correct?"

"Yes. That's perfect." Janet often tried to work a day ahead, a habit that made her job less frantic.

"You can count on us." Mom and Becca carted the last things to their cars as the first coffee customers came through the front door. As the mothers pulled away, Harry came in, with a fully restored Crosby trotting happily at his side.

"Be still my heart," Debbie whispered beside her, and Janet's heart echoed the words. To see Harry walking with his beloved friend on this milder day was a blessing.

When he saw them, Harry smiled.

"Oh, it's good to see both of you back to your old selves." Janet smiled a welcome, her hands busy with frosting elements.

"Eggs over easy and toast today, Harry?" Debbie asked. Janet could tell she tried to sound nonchalant, but there was no mistaking the warm welcome in her voice.

"Yes, ma'am. Exactly that. Thank you."

And that was all it took to make a crazy start to the day better.

Seeing Harry and Crosby, both healthy and content, put things in perspective.

They were better, the mothers had come to Janet's rescue, and the storm warning for tomorrow had been canceled. A warm front pushing up from the Gulf was sending drier air their way for the next couple of days. Her father was still planning to put up the tent with the help of Debbie's dad and a couple of friends, but it was a relief to know the weather wasn't going to be the washout they'd expected.

Allie arrived slightly before eight o'clock. After carefully examining the oven, she stood and walked to the sink to wash her hands. "Bad igniter," she announced.

"I have no idea what that means, but it sounds expensive," said Debbie.

"It would be except that your father bought an appliance repair contract for the business when you guys opened your doors," Allie told her cheerfully. "He said unexpected repairs are a new business's worst nightmare and that you'd never let him pay for them."

"He was right." Debbie folded her arms, unamused.

"Regardless, you have a contract on all equipment that I can fix, which is pretty much everything you've got here except the deep fryer, but it takes a lot to kill those. And even on that I can do some repairs. So I'll order this, have it shipped from Cleveland, and we'll have you back up and running tomorrow. Okay?"

"That's wonderful." Janet nudged Debbie. "And what a thoughtful thing for your dad to do." She fixed an extra-hot chai latte for Allie and handed it to her once she'd packed up her tools and reloaded her car. "On the house. Thanks for coming right over."

Allie sniffed the spiced aroma of the hot tea. "Anytime. I love the perks of coming here. No pun intended. And don't be too hard on your dad," she said to Debbie with a wink. "If nothing had gone bad, you'd never have known he did it, but he's a numbers guy. He ran a tight ship at Good Shepherd, and he knows the importance of a good backup plan."

"I won't yell at him," Debbie replied as she refilled the coffee maker. "I'll hug him. He'll like that better." She winked at Allie.

Harry beamed at them as Patricia came in the door. "Family." He grinned at his granddaughter. "In the end, it's all about God and family, isn't it? And a good dog."

"I'll add a tall peppermint mocha to that list." Patricia slung an arm around Harry's shoulders and planted a kiss on his cheek. "You look so much better, Pop Pop! Good to see you out and about again."

"And I feel the same, so that's a good day right there. Faith, family, and friends."

Janet had to agree. She refilled his coffee before starting Patricia's drink, and as the Franklins talked about their weekend plans, she smiled.

Harry had the recipe right. Faith, family, and friends. And if a great little café added good food and fun to the mix, that was a pretty good deal.

She prayed it would give her the strength to solve the mystery of Sadie's family.

Kielce, Poland
October 1942

Dearest sister,

My summer note failed to reach you. I know this because it had to be destroyed so it wouldn't fall into the wrong hands, so I write again now to tell you of our life here. Joseph works on, so clever with the running of trains. He has a route that takes him north and south with occasional stops at home, but with the busy-ness of the time, those stops are infrequent now.

My work here continues, as I am hired to put my talents with needle and thread to use on a regular basis. In return I am allowed to keep our home here and the small garden plot. The farm is now run by a family brought in from another place. It is odd not to be working the land.

Fuel is scarce and winter looms once more, but I have a solid roof and thick walls, and one of the women put in a fuel allowance for us. She insisted that I cannot stitch with frozen fingers, and her words rang true. Coal was delivered the next day, and a load of wood was brought by as well. I will parcel it out because Polish winters are long, windy, and cold, but it is a relief to have a chance at warmth.

Another woman has been bringing a small basket of food each week. The baskets grow meager, so it seems their rations may also be running low of late. It is hard to know, but she has two sturdy boys, eleven and twelve years of age, and we all know that boys need food to grow.

I have finished two blankets from remnants left with me by the women whose fashions I now mend and make. I have sent one on to you, done in shades of taupe, ivory, and gold. It is a subtle covering. The colors do not sing with joy, but they offer quiet harmony to one another. As a lover of song, I believe you will enjoy this attribute. One of the women who frequents my door advised a splash of berry red, but I chose quieter tones. Let me know what you think, dear one, for you know I value your opinion most highly.

I am sending this out with hopes that it reaches you, but if not, I shall write again. Our correspondence is our only connection. It is quite dear to me.

May God's blessings abound for you and yours, dear Nessie!

Your loving sister,

Anya

CHAPTER SIXTEEN

With Mom and Becca's help, Janet had the next day's orders packaged and labeled by closing time. She and Debbie cleaned up quickly. Paulette had stayed to help, and she was going to work longer shifts on Friday and Saturday to cover tables while Janet made doughnut dough and filled bakery orders. Paulette tapped the order rack as she passed it and whistled softly. "Many hands make light work, don't they?"

"Yes." Janet had cleaned the big mixer and was polishing the work surfaces before they headed to That's My Baby. "And having you here has made things easier for both of us, Paulette. You're an asset to this café, and we probably don't tell you that often enough."

Paulette laughed. "Well, you pay me, so that's something, right?"

Debbie acknowledged that with a smile. "Never a bad thing."

Paulette tugged her jacket off a hook and headed out.

Janet hung her apron and reached for her own jacket. "Are we driving together?"

Debbie shook her head. "Afterward, I need to drop off some things at the library and a container of soup for Harry. Let's drive separate."

Janet pulled into the doll repair shop's driveway a few minutes later. Sadie's car was there, and Debbie was climbing out of hers.

They let themselves in the front door, and Sadie called from the back, "I'm in the kitchen."

Sadie had set up tea and coffee, and Janet was surprised when she walked into the room. Generally, the little kitchen was cluttered. Not because Sadie was messy, but because there hadn't been the time to get it in shape before.

Apparently, Sadie had found the time. Today the room looked welcoming. Janet whistled softly. "Sadie, this cleaned up so nicely. I love how this table fits into this nook. It's like it was made for it. And that stenciling is darling." Someone had stenciled a farmhouse scene on each side of the table. It was worn in spots, but charming.

"It's taken all these months to clean up the place and figure things out. I called Greg Connor about updating the upstairs living space, like I mentioned before. Debbie, he said he'd recently done some work for you." She set out a pretty cup filled with spoons and an old-fashioned sugar bowl. "He said I should ask you about it. Would you recommend Greg? We've never had anything major done here or at our house, so this is new territory for me."

Sadie didn't seem to notice the light flush that stained Debbie's cheeks, but Janet did.

Debbie set her purse on the small counter nearby and slipped into a chair. "He did great work. I'd absolutely recommend him."

"That's what everyone says. Good." Sadie started to pour coffee. The jingle of the bell over the front door made her pause.

"You pour." Janet headed out front. "I'll get it." She went through the short swinging door and found Martin Janek waiting in the front of the shop. She was relieved to see that he resembled the man in the online photo today, rather than the angry man they'd met the week before.

She moved forward. "Mr. Janek." She held out her hand in welcome. "Sadie and Debbie are in the kitchen. I'm Janet Shaw. Debbie Albright and I own the new café at the depot."

She thought he'd acknowledge knowing that.

He didn't. "I didn't know the old place shut down."

Janet led the way to the kitchen. "Over a year ago. My friend and I bought it, and it's a café and bakery now."

He nodded politely, and nothing about his countenance seemed less than sincere, so was someone else leaving the notes on their cars?

But if it wasn't him, who could it be?

Sadie came forward when they walked through the swinging door. Janet was pretty sure her friend's confident air was an act, but she did it well. "Mr. Janek?"

He cringed. "Please, it's Martin. I'm not fancy."

Sadie's gaze softened. "We aren't either."

He took a deep breath as if bracing himself, and then his features relaxed. "I'm sorry I busted in here like I did last time. It was wrong, and I'm afraid I made a terrible first impression on you."

Sadie motioned to a chair. "Have a seat. Please."

They sat down as Sadie raised the coffeepot. "Can I pour you some coffee or tea? Or would you like water?"

"Water's good, thanks. I can't do coffee so late in the day anymore." His gravelly tone could have been mistaken for old age if he weren't sitting right in front of them. He was clearly not old, probably in his midsixties or so.

Sadie filled a glass with ice water and set it in front of him.

"Thank you," he told her. "Listen, about last time?"

All three women leaned in.

"I was out of line. My wife told me exactly how out of line I was." He gave a small smile then sobered again. "But when you're raised knowing something, and you see it played out in front of you and your family day after day, it eats at you, you know?"

Sadie shook her head. "I *don't* know, actually. I didn't have a clue what you were talking about the first time you were here. I had no idea what made you so angry or what I'd done wrong. I still don't."

"Not you, of course." He jutted his chin in her direction. "You're mixed up in this through no fault of your own, same as me. But when it's gone on for generations, there's a lot of dirt that gets swept under the rug. Unless you're like my wife, who makes sure to roll up the rugs and clean under them now and again." He reached out and lifted the pretty mug holding the spoons. "This."

"What about it?" Sadie asked.

"Pretty, right?" Appreciation for the intricately designed mug was evident in his voice. "Hand-painted or stamped."

"It was my grandmother's," Sadie told him. "She inherited it from her mother. She had a set of them, but one broke. She cried when it happened." She sobered. "I haven't thought of that in a long time—how sad she was over that cup. It was accidentally knocked off the counter after a big family meal. Everything was cluttered with too many dishes, and the cup hit the floor and shattered beyond repair. Oh, her face." She ran a finger over the cup that had survived. "Yes, it's beautiful."

"Heritage." He said the word softly. "Our heritage, Sadie. Yours and mine."

Sadie frowned. "I don't understand. I guessed that we must be related. I remember my grandmother saying the name Janek once, but I don't know why. And where does a beautiful cup fit in?"

He handed it to her. "Read the bottom."

Uncertainty flickered over Sadie's face, but she obeyed. "'Made in Poland.'"

"Right. That's where we come from. With other stuff mixed in now, of course. But the Janeks and the Oleskis came out of Poland, both before and after World War II."

"Oleskis?" Janet was busy typing notes into her phone.

Martin took the cup back from Sadie. "Your great-grandparents changed their names to Joe and Annie Harper and told everyone they were from Ireland. They denied their Polish roots and broke my grandpa's heart. My father was angry. So angry." He set down the cup and folded his hands on the table, a working man's hands. "He died carrying that resentment, and that's not how I want to live. My father loved his father. He knew what was sacrificed and how many were killed during that war. Family, friends, neighbors. When your great-grandparents denied their heritage and changed their names, he was devastated. He knew why they did it too, and that made it worse."

Janet exchanged a glance with Debbie. Neither of them had gotten a chance to tell Sadie what they'd learned from Violet and Eileen about her grandmother's unconscious utterings and her great-grandfather's accent. Martin's revelation wasn't as surprising to them as it obviously was to their friend.

"I'm not aware of name changes or anything else about this." Sadie appeared shocked, and for good reason. Martin Janek was blowing up her family history. "Why would they do such a thing?"

"The jewels."

"What jewels?"

"When they heard rumors of what was happening in Germany, everyone in the family gave their jewelry to your great-grand-mother—Anya—for safekeeping. As I said, you knew her as Annie Harper. Annie and Joe *Harper* from Ireland." He stressed the sur-name. "But they were really Anya and Joseph *Oleski* from Poland. Those were their real names."

Sadie's face was pale and still. She'd locked her gaze on Martin and seemed unable to look away as he shredded the little she knew of her family.

He clearly understood what he was doing and seemed to regret it. But he continued to speak, his voice gentle. "According to my grandfather, Anya's sister, Ernestine, and her husband, George Ostrowski, left Poland in 1938 and came to America. My grandfa-ther followed in 1940. Anya and Joseph stayed in Poland to take care of things, but by the war's end, there wasn't much left to care for. The farm had been all but destroyed by the soldiers that occupied the area, so the land wasn't valuable as it had once been. That part wasn't their fault. My father used to say how everyone trusted Anya and Joe because they had hearts of gold."

Sadie's lip trembled. "They did. How did they survive?"

"The railroad kept Joseph on, even after Germany took over, because he knew his stuff. My understanding is that that was their main source of income, though Anya also did some sewing work.

When the war was over and they came to America, the family eventually saw their true colors. Joseph's and Anya's."

"What do you mean?" Sadie asked. The words were choked, as if she struggled to get them out.

"They changed their names." His face turned red with anger. "They came to America and didn't tell anyone. My family didn't even know they were in the country until twenty-five years after they arrived. They had spent years writing to Anya with no answer, and finally faced the fact that she and her family had likely not survived the war. They grieved the loss for over two decades. Joseph and Anya might never have been discovered if not for my grandmother seeing your grandmother working at a Mennonite store north of here. She knew right away who she was. She was the spitting image of my great-great-grandmother—pale skin, pale eyes, pale hair."

"Grandma Mary," Sadie whispered.

He winced. "Her name wasn't Mary. Not to my family. Her name was Marysia. Marysia Ilaina Oleski."

CHAPTER SEVENTEEN

arysia?" Sadie held his gaze, surprised.

"In Poland she was Marysia. Her parents sent her off to a school in Lisbon before the war came. My family never heard about or saw her again until my grandmother came face-to-face with her in Sugarcreek. My grandmother called her by name and told her she was so sorry about her parents and how much they all missed Anya and Joseph."

Sadie covered her mouth with one hand.

"This beautiful young woman, with a scarf tied around her head just like her grandmother would have done, looked straight at her and said, 'I'm sorry. You must have the wrong person. I'm Mary Harper from Dennison, and my parents are Joe and Annie Harper. They didn't die in the war.' It broke my grandmother's heart. Either Marysia legitimately didn't know the truth and had lost their heritage, or she was a cold customer."

"How sad," Debbie murmured.

Martin circled the glass of water with his hands. "My grandmother came home weeping. My grandfather wanted to know what was wrong, and she told him what had happened. My grandfather was furious. He and my father went to find the Harpers in Dennison. Sure enough, they were Joseph and Anya Oleski. Grandfather accused them of being thieves. They wouldn't say what they'd done with the jewels except that they'd been put to good use. My grandfather spat on the floor and told them they were dead to him—for real this time. Then he made a show of kicking the dust off his shoes as he went out the door. And that was the last we ever saw of them, as far as I know."

Sadie took a deep, shuddering breath.

"I'm sorry," Martin said. "I realized after I barged in here that you had no idea what I was talking about, and I'm sorry to be the one to tell you everything and flip your world upside down. My children wouldn't forgive me if I carried a family grudge like this, because this isn't our way. It's never been our way."

"What brought this to the surface, Martin?" Debbie asked. "The doll?"

He raised an eyebrow in surprise. "No. All the kids had rag dolls like that. My grandmother made them, and hers before her, she said. A 'floppy doll,' she called it. Easy for little ones to hang on to. No, it was the trunk. My grandmother had one like it, but smaller. And Anya's sister, Ernestine had one too, the biggest one. They all fit inside each other. You know, like those Russian dolls?"

All three women nodded.

"My great-great-grandfather, Chester Janek, made them and gave one to Anya, one to Ernestine, and one to my grandmother. She wasn't a Janek by birth, but she had married my grandfather by that time, and Chester was very fond of her. It was a tangible way for them all to stay connected as a family, no matter where they ended up."

"That's beautiful," Janet said.

"When my grandparents left Poland for America, all the cousins said that someday they would meet and put the trunks together like they should be. Like we should be. That never happened. When Anya and Joseph came, they denied their heritage and wouldn't even acknowledge their family. When I saw the trunk in that photo, all I could see was the anger and heartbreak my father and grandfather went through because of their betrayal. I went ballistic, and I'm sorry about that. It will never happen again. I promise."

Empathy deepened Sadie's expression. She pressed her lips into a thin line and then said, "I had no idea, and I'm truly sorry for how it hurt you and your family. But you mentioned Ernestine." Sadie sat up straighter and exchanged glances with Debbie and Janet. "Are you referring to Nessie?"

He shrugged. "Maybe. My family lost touch with her after the war."

"That's what my grandmother called her sister," Sadie explained. "It must be the same person. I never met her. Gigi said they lost touch over the years. We just found out that Grandma Mary lived with Nessie in New York during the war."

"So she wasn't at a school in Lisbon," Martin said. "They sent her to America."

Janet raised her head from her phone, where she was making notes. "I'm confused about something. You said the family gave Anya their jewelry before the war for safekeeping. Why didn't they get it back from her before they moved here?"

"They'd heard stories about people being robbed on the ships," Martin said. "They feared that soldiers or thieves would seize anything they found, anything not hidden well. Anya and Joe had plenty of hiding spots on the farm, and everyone expected them to come to America when the war was over, when it would be safer to travel with valuables. My grandfather accused them of stealing because they never gave the jewelry back. They said they didn't have it anymore, but they wouldn't say what they did with it."

"Do you know what the jewelry looked like?" Sadie asked.

"Grandfather had a list," he replied. "Let's see…" He closed his eyes in thought. "My great-aunt's sapphire necklace. A couple of other gold necklaces. My grandmother's diamond ring. An emerald brooch that was passed down for several generations." He opened his eyes. "I can't remember anything else. Of course, my grandparents and great-grandparents are gone now. My father too. So there's really no one left for me to ask about it."

"Do you have any pictures of the jewelry?" Janet asked, acutely aware of the brooch in particular. Perhaps they'd finally learned the history of the emerald brooch Sadie had found inside the rag doll. "Maybe of someone wearing the brooch or one of the necklaces?"

"No, unfortunately. When the Germans came, most folks lost everything. So many people were driven out by the Russians or the Germans, and then the Germans sent the Russians packing. Who knows what happened to anything?" He shrugged. "I figure if people came out of it alive, more power to them, and that's how I should have approached you to begin with. I saw that trunk and thought the worst, and that was wrong of me."

"I'm sorry it brought up so many bad old feelings." Sadie took his hand. "But I'm glad you came to talk it out, to tell us the story. I don't know where the truth lies in any of it, but I know that my family has never had what we'd call extra money. They worked hard their whole lives, and I never heard anything about jewels." She hesitated.

Janet glanced at Debbie. They were probably all wondering the same thing—was it time to tell Martin about the emerald brooch?

Sadie gave them a small nod and sat back. "When I cleaned out the attic, I found an emerald brooch inside the doll. The one that was in the photo with the trunk."

"Inside the doll?" Martin echoed. "Who would do that?"

"I don't know," Sadie confessed. "The trunk was here, and the doll was in the trunk. I haven't seen any other jewels, certainly nothing like the ones you mentioned. The police chief has the brooch now. I wanted it kept safe until we found out more about it."

"Why would anyone hide something like that in a scruffy old doll?" Martin asked.

"To smuggle it? For safekeeping?" Sadie guessed. "And maybe it was so well hidden, it was forgotten?"

"If it's the one that your family gave to Anya," Janet cut in, "what was it doing in a trunk that Nessie brought from Poland in 1938? Did Nessie know it was there?"

"Maybe Annie gave it to Nessie before Nessie left for America," Sadie suggested.

"Well, we're all descendants of whoever owned the brooch," Martin said. "So I don't think it was so much that my grandfather wanted it back. I think the problem was the shattered trust. That your great-grandparents came here, changed their names, and let everyone think they were dead. And it was only by chance they were discovered. Or by God's will."

"Did your trunk have anything like that in it?" Debbie asked. "A rag doll or something similar? I'm wondering if the look-alike trunks each carried some of the family's treasures inside."

"Ours held linens for years, and then my wife brought it downstairs to sit next to the fireplace when we added a room about twenty years back. We keep games and toys in it for when our grandkids visit. As far as I know, there's never been any old dolls or jewelry in it." Martin stood and offered one hand to Sadie. "Either way, it was a long time ago. My faith and my heart don't allow me to hold a grudge about the past. Please forgive my harsh words. It won't happen again."

Sadie stepped around his hand and hugged him instead. "We're cousins. Maybe distant ones, but family nevertheless. It's good to know you and good to know this story. I'm glad to know your family's side of what happened. We'll keep investigating," she promised. "All three of us. We want to find out why the brooch was in the doll. I can't imagine my great-grandparents were thieves, but I want to know the whole truth about that jewelry. And what happened in Poland, now that we've got the right country. Did you know that my grandmother went searching for her roots when she was a young woman? Roots she couldn't find?"

"Roots that didn't exist in Ireland because she wasn't Irish," he guessed immediately.

"Exactly. If nothing else, I owe it to Grandma Mary to figure out as much as I can. Do you want us to keep you in the loop?"

"Nothing would make me happier. And not because I want anything," he assured her. "But knowing would be good. No matter what it is," he stressed. "War is an awful thing, and folks do what they need to do to stay alive. I can't imagine dealing with that myself, but I'd love it if you and I could heal the terrible effects generations later."

"I feel the same way," Sadie told him. She walked Martin to the exit, flipped the sign to Closed, and locked the door. Then she came back to the kitchen. "Well."

"I'll say." Janet gripped her mug with both hands. "This puts a whole new spin on things, doesn't it?"

"Mary knew something was wrong." Debbie got up and set her mug in the sink.

"Do you think it was because of Martin's grandmother's reaction to her?"

"It could be," said Janet. "Or she heard her parents talking about his grandfather's visit to their home."

Janet considered all of that for a moment. "So Estelle, Eileen, and now Martin have all said that Marysia was sent over before the war."

Sadie nodded as Debbie scribbled a crude timeline on a piece of paper.

"Anya and Joe stayed in Poland for the farm."

"Yes."

"Maybe Anya sewed the brooch into Mary's doll so that it wouldn't get taken?" Debbie tapped the pencil against her mouth. "Because it had sentimental value?"

"But then why put the doll in a trunk and forget about it?" Janet asked. "Wouldn't you remove the brooch?"

"Maybe Anya wasn't the one who put it in the trunk," said Sadie. "It was Nessie's trunk, after all. Maybe Nessie put the doll in there, not knowing what was inside."

"But there was mail service. Telegrams. And then phone and long distance, so if Anya was searching for the brooch, she'd have contacted her sister. Wouldn't she?" Janet asked. "I get how things get lost, but if this was special enough to hide in a doll, it makes no sense that Anya didn't follow up on it." She paused. "By the way, what should we call them? Should we use their Polish names or their Americanized versions?"

"I say we use the names they chose for themselves," Sadie said. "We might never know what was going on, but I trust them. I trust the goodness I heard about them."

Janet laid a hand on her friend's arm. "I do too. They got out alive. We can't sit in judgment of their situation. Now we know they were in Poland, not Ireland. Knowing how many died and were displaced in that takeover puts me in a different frame of mind. How many people do we know who have suffered from acts of war?"

"Drew lost his uncle in Desert Storm." Sadie tugged her sweater a little closer. "His grandmother was never the same after that. And you know what this means firsthand." Compassion filled her gaze as she focused on Debbie.

"I do," Debbie answered quietly. Janet appreciated Sadie's thoughtfulness. Debbie had lost her fiancé twenty years before in Afghanistan.

"So let's keep searching." Janet put on her jacket as she spoke. "Let's figure out what the connection is with our anonymous email friend and whoever is putting notes on our cars. Because neither one of them is Martin."

Debbie agreed as they moved toward the door. "He opened a door for us today, but we've still got a lot of locked windows. We'll open them, Sadie. One by one, if we have to."

Janet tucked her phone into her pocket. "For the next couple of days we'll be bogged down in doughnuts, St. Patrick's Day, and Tiffany's birthday. But Monday brings a whole new week. We'll be able to tackle this with renewed focus then. Or at the very least with fewer distractions."

"Although Easter is two weeks away," Debbie reminded her. "And thus begins another busy season!"

Janet laughed as they stepped outside. "I love every minute, though," she told Debbie as Sadie relocked the door behind them. "Being busy, planning holidays, being in charge with you. Don't get me wrong. I loved working at the Third Street Bakery, and they gave me a solid background in commercial baking. But there's nothing like running your own business and making your own decisions with your best friend. And if a little mystery takes us slightly off course? That's the frosting on the cake."

She and Debbie said their goodbyes, and then Janet hurried home. Tiffany was working on her dresser in the basement. Ian texted that he'd be an hour late. Janet was serving breakfast for dinner, so she had a little time for some sleuthing.

She sat down at her laptop and called her mother to change the online ancestry search from Irish Harper to Polish Oleski. When they tried that, the adjustment made a significant difference in results. But, although several Oleski descendants had developed family trees online, none of them linked to Anya and Joseph.

"How can there be nothing?" Janet complained to her mother half an hour later. "With so many people finding connections through DNA registries and ancestry sites, this seems abnormal, doesn't it?"

"Two world wars and a Great Depression mess up family trees, sweetie." Like always, Mom kept it simple. "People look back at the fifties with a lot of nostalgia. But many immigrants from invaded countries came here after seeing and experiencing unspeakable evil at the hands of others. It's not surprising that they didn't know who they could trust. They worked hard and kept to themselves because it was hard to know friend from foe for a while."

"I never thought of it that way." Janet minimized the website and stood. She took the phone to the kitchen to start laying out bacon. "I assumed that after a major war like that, people would welcome each other with open arms."

"Some did. Many didn't. Worries about jobs and finances and education and economic effect took their toll." Janet heard a voice in the background. "Gotta go, darling. Your dad's calling. I'll talk to you later, okay?"

"Thanks, Mom." Janet ended the call. She understood what her mother had said.

Assimilation wasn't easy. Transitions could be hard. Perhaps the Harpers hadn't done anything wrong in Europe. Maybe they'd come to the land of the free and home of the brave only to face discrimination, then changed their names to ward off prejudice. But even if that was true, why didn't they try to find their relatives?

Tiffany dashed up the basement steps, carrying two small paintbrushes in her hand. Her eyes lit up when she entered the kitchen. "Bacon!"

Janet laughed. "I knew you'd come running when you smelled it cooking."

Tiffany began washing her brushes in the sink, scrubbing the bristles with her fingers as the water sluiced a teal-toned paint down the drain. "They make bacon at school too, but not like yours. Never like yours."

"Not like mine either?" Ian kicked off his boots and came through the door, grinning.

"You mean burnt beyond all recognition?" Tiffany joked. "No, they've got that one covered, actually. An advanced part of my education was realizing there are people who actually like burnt bacon."

"Extra crispy and slightly charred is the best way to do it." Ian winked at her and grabbed a can of soda from the refrigerator.

"Cooking it in the oven is a lot less messy." Janet slid the cooling tray of bacon to one side. "But some folks around here don't like change."

Ian planted a kiss on her cheek. "Takes too long that way. But it does come out perfect. Every time." He snagged a piece as he headed upstairs. "Grabbing a shower. See you in ten."

"I told Gramps I'd help him tomorrow," Tiffany announced as she split bagels for the toaster. "He pretended they didn't need help, but I know how fumble-fingered they get with the packaging, and I love working events like Doughnut Days. So many of the people that come by have stories to share. I told Gramps I'd stay until two, and he gave me a monster-sized hug."

"Grandma and Gramps miss you."

"I know. I miss them too." Tiffany went to the refrigerator and pulled out the eggs. She took six out of the carton and said, "One of my future roommates in the apartment is from Chicago, and she's a vegetarian. She's all excited because she found a store close to where we're going to be that has eggs from cage-free chickens." Tiffany laughed as she broke the eggs into a bowl. "I told her that in Dennison we always get our eggs from cage-free chickens."

Janet smiled at her. "The Suttons' hobby farm has kept us supplied for years."

And then Tiffany's words powered on a light bulb in Janet's brain.

There was another place to get cage-free eggs not far from Dennison. And Mary Harper had worked at the general store that sold them. Would someone there know more about her? And if they did, would they share that information with her and Debbie?

A trip to Sugarcreek was definitely in Janet's near future.

Kielce, Poland
December 1942

Nessie, my dear, a blessed Christmas be yours!

I am sending this via my beloved Joseph on the first of the month because the journey of any missive these days can be long and arduous.

I dreamed last night.

Oh, what a dream, dear Nessie!

I remembered Papa coming in from the barn and carrying that tiny pair of lambs, born too soon. Remember, sweet sister? Our big, rugged father striding in, snow and all, with Mama scolding him every inch of the way until she saw what he carried.

It was as if her scolding melted on sight, wasn't it? She quickly made something for the wee ones to drink. In my dream I saw her stoke the fire to warm the mixture before she tucked those babies into a nest made by chairs. There they stayed for several days while the mother sheep bleated outside.

Remember Papa's words?

He said that hearing her voice would help the babies to strengthen, for they would want to be with her. He explained that her voice inspired them to grow, and their plaintive calls helped her body ready milk for nursing them.

The bond between mother and child is profound, is it not?

And in this particular month, this particular time, the thought of mother and child is such a poignant reminder of what Mary did for the Christ child.

Being a good parent, a good mother, has always been my goal. I know it is true for you as well. I pray for your family every day, and for you. My hope is that provisions for all of the children are sufficient, even if just enough. I have learned that excess is a thing best avoided, for it is not needed and makes us forget gratitude.

God has given me so much to be grateful for! The generous spirits I've found in you and others, keeping warm with the work of my hands while your work shapes a nation. It is a beautiful circle, stitched with the wealth of old and love anew.

Hallelujah, dear sister. Hallelujah. God be with you, with all of you!

Your loving sister,

Anya

CHAPTER EIGHTEEN

The new tent required some wrestling and assistance from both Greg and Ian, but they managed to get it up as Allie arrived to fix the oven in time for Friday's opening. Janet counted that a major success.

They enjoyed two days of record-breaking doughnut sales. The tent was a hit, and their well-shared social media campaign pushed café sales to an all-time high. Regular customers came by, along with a wave of brand-new people. Orders were filled, and the bakery case sold a wide array of Celtic-themed cupcakes and cookies and even a few key lime pies.

It was wonderful. Janet let herself into the café on Monday morning, expecting to enjoy a proper catch-up day.

But as so often happened, things didn't work out that way.

While the oven was working great, the dishwasher chugged to a stop midmorning.

"I forgot how tedious handwashing can be," Janet whispered to Debbie as Paulette hurried lunch orders back and forth to the six occupied tables. It wasn't crazy busy on the floor, but eight to-go orders had come in from the trade school in Uhrichsville.

"At least these don't leave extra dishes," Debbie noted as she built a variety of wraps on the counter.

"There's a blessing in that, for sure." Janet finished drying the last of the current dish load as Greg came through the door.

"I heard there was a little problem here, ma'am?" He smiled at Debbie and hefted his toolbox. "Might have exactly what you need right here."

"A girl can dream," she replied with a sigh. "The dishwasher stopped working. I didn't know if we should call you or Allie's Appliance because I wasn't sure what the problem was. It seems to be in the plumbing. Or the draining. Definitely water-related."

"I'm glad you called." He came around the counter. "I hope you know you can call me anytime. Okay?"

Debbie nodded.

Janet had been Debbie's friend long enough to know that little things mattered to her. Debbie wasn't a flashy person. She didn't like a lot of attention, but she appreciated thoughtful acts. Greg's kindness in coming over at once was one of those thoughtful acts.

He checked the machine over while Janet ladled soup from the warming station. "The pump's bad. I'll order a new one. We should be able to get it in by tomorrow."

"So I should have called Allie first?" Debbie asked. "I thought for sure it was a plumbing problem when things backed up. And we've got that contract with her, thanks to Dad."

"You were right to call me first." He grinned up at her from his spot on the floor. "Allie's great, but I hope I rank higher on your speed dial than the local appliance shop. Besides, I think I heard her mention something about being fully booked this week."

She flushed, though a smile broke over her face.

"The boys are both signed up for the Cy Young baseball camp in Newcomerstown next weekend." He moved to the sink to wash his hands while Debbie packed the wraps and sandwiches into their to-go containers. "Ian and I think it would be the perfect time to take you two out for a Saturday night on the town." He dried his hands and pitched the paper towel into the garbage can nearby. "Even if our town is a little on the small side. What do you think?"

"Hanging out with my three best friends?" Janet swiped her flour-dusted hands on her second-favorite train apron. "I'm in."

Debbie hesitated, but Greg didn't seem put off. His smile grew teasing, and his eyes twinkled at Debbie. "We can call it supper with friends." He picked up the toolbox. "I'm fine with that. For now." He winked and headed for the door. "Call me later and let me know, okay?"

Debbie fastened the lid onto the dish containing their signature chicken salad then tucked it into the cooler. "No need to call. I'd love to go. We'll have a wonderful time."

Greg beamed. "We sure will. I'll bring that pump by as soon as it comes in."

When Greg was out the door, Janet nudged Debbie's shoulder. "A date?"

"A fun night with friends, and maybe not as scary as I would have thought. I'm not into messing up kids' emotions to figure out what might or might not be there between Greg and me." She refilled the sink with hot, soapy water. "But Julian seems to like me well enough, and that's real sweet. Jaxon, on the other hand..." She grimaced. "He misses his mother. And I don't want to be insensitive to that."

Stepping into uncharted waters had never been easy for Debbie, and a guy with two teenage sons doubled the risk. Four hearts would be affected, rather than two. She was wise to step carefully. "Well, I've found you likable since we teamed up to race Duane Goodson on our bikes and you blocked him so I could win."

"And then you returned the favor, and Duane went home crying."

"I'd forgotten that part." Janet swirled buttery-yellow frosting onto chocolate cupcakes with a frown. "That was kind of mean of us, wasn't it?"

"We were four," Debbie reminded her. "We've improved."

"And Duane has a good job up in New Philadelphia, with a really nice wife and three kids, so I guess we didn't scar him for life," Janet noted. She closed the six-pack of cupcakes, slid it to the side, and started another tray. "Think we'll make it to Stutzman's by three like we wanted to?"

"I can stay and do the dishes," Paulette said, coming through the kitchen door with a couple more orders. "I have nothing going on at home, the boys' basketball season is over, baseball season doesn't start for a while yet, and I'm bored. I'd actually be glad to do it."

"I'm never one to refuse a good deed," Janet said.

Paulette's kindness gave them the allowance they needed to get up to Sugarcreek. When they entered Stutzman's, Janet's immediate thought was that there was nothing typical about this place. The store was filled with everything a person would need to keep a well-stocked pantry, and they carried most things in bulk or simple packaging. She loved that.

"Whoa." Debbie paused inside the door and ogled the wide expanse of loaded shelves. "I'm in love."

"Isn't it wonderful?" Janet crossed to the checkout area. "Hello," she said to the middle-aged woman behind the counter.

The woman smiled at her. "Hello," she said. "My name is Hannah. Is there something I can help you find?"

"This is a wonderful store, Hannah," Janet said, "and I'm sure I'll buy something before I leave, but we came to see if there's anyone still at the store who might have known a woman named Mary Harper."

"Why, yes, I remember Mary," Hannah said. "She came to work here long before I did, and she retired almost twenty years ago. I did not get to work with her for very long. But Mrs. Stutzman is here today, working on the books, and I am sure she would not mind talking to you. She knew Mary much better than I did."

"That would be a great help," Debbie told her.

"My pleasure." Hannah pointed the way to a small corridor. "Knock on the door, and she will call you in. She is hard of hearing but denies it, so speak up, all right?"

"We will. Thank you, Hannah." Janet smiled at her.

They wove through the aisles to the rear corner of the spacious store. Janet knocked.

No one answered.

"Hard of hearing, remember?" Debbie whispered, and Janet knocked louder.

"*Kumme.*"

Janet opened the door, and she and Debbie stepped into a warehouse area. On their left was a small, well-lit office. Glass panels allowed a full view of the warehouse from inside the office.

The large, organized stocking area splayed out to their right. Industrial-strength shelving was filled with neatly labeled items, ready to supply the busy store behind them. A big cooler took up the far corner, adjacent to a door leading to the parking lot, where horses and buggies as well as a few bicycles were parked. Beyond that was another lot filled with cars and trucks.

"*Ja?*" A woman emerged from the office. She was small, and her quick movements reminded Janet of a cartoon chipmunk Tiffany had loved as a child. The woman peered at them over the edge of her rimless glasses. "I am Susannah Stutzman. Have you come to see me?"

Janet stepped forward. "I'm Janet Shaw, Mrs. Stutzman. And this is my friend Debbie Albright. We own the café at the depot in Dennison."

Mrs. Stutzman tipped the glasses down, examining Janet more carefully. "Lorilee is your *mater*?"

"Yes."

"A *gut* cook and baker, like her mater before her," the elderly woman declared. "She would come to the store long ago, and she would bring the little one along."

"Thank you. My mother has great memories of coming here with Grandma, and I remember her bringing me along and getting me a candy stick from the jars. If I was good, that is," Janet added with a laugh.

"A tradition one passes down." Mrs. Stutzman beamed. "Come in. It is chilly out here. Although the days are getting nicer, eh?" Janet and Debbie followed Mrs. Stutzman into the small office. Two folding chairs were drawn up to a cluttered desk. Mrs. Stutzman moved around the desk, took a seat, and then folded her hands in her lap.

There was an open laptop on the desk. Mrs. Stutzman must have caught Janet's confusion, because she pointed to it and lifted a brow. "You are possibly wondering why we have such things?"

Janet's mouth dropped open. "Um, no. Of course not. And it's not my place to wonder such things."

"I will tell you anyway. We are not Amish," Mrs. Stutzman explained. "We are Mennonite. We run a big business here, for which I hire English and Amish and Mennonite workers, and my soul magnifies the Lord. We are from Walnut Creek."

Walnut Creek was a lovely town about ten minutes away.

"We use electric to keep things going, but we often use our buggy or bicycles to get from place to place. We remember our roots in an Amish church as children, but my parents and Malcolm's parents helped build the Mennonite church up the road. We are strict in some ways and open in others. But we all work together in these beautiful towns so that people come. They buy, they have fellowship, and they pray. We make a difference."

"That is wonderful. Thank you for explaining," Janet said as she settled into the chair.

"Certainly. Now, what can I do for you?"

Debbie got right to the point. "Mrs. Stutzman, we came to ask you about a woman who worked here many years ago. Her name was Mary Harper, and we were told she worked here for a long time. Do you remember her?"

"*Ach*, remember?" Mrs. Stutzman's expression softened. "She was a blessing. She was here when we bought the business, and I took to her right off." She sighed. "But she had not had an easy life, I could tell. Some days she was good at a calm face, you know." She motioned with her hands. "Not showing her feelings. But there were a few times when she wept as if her heart would break."

With a vague idea why, Janet couldn't blame Mary for that.

"When her *maam* died, she came to work as if it was any other day, but it was not, of course. It was a day of grieving and loss, so we sent her home, but she came back. Her eyes were red, and her mouth trembled, but she walked in here, took her apron off the hook, and tied it on. Then she faced me with such determination that I was surprised. You would not think such a pale little thing could be so strong, but she was. She stood here in this office, squared her shoulders, and said, 'They gave me away once and never told me why. Being part of this business means more to me than a home that cast out a little girl without even a second thought.'"

Part of that jumped out at Janet. "She felt cast out because they sent her to America to be safe?"

Mrs. Stutzman studied her face. "I have raised six children," she told them. "I have seventeen grandchildren and a few great-grandchildren now. In my time with so many, I know that each is different. God has made them so. What was right and good for one will not work for all. Mary's difficulty was that she wanted to know about her past. That was not merely discouraged in her family. It was forbidden. We know ourselves here. My family knows where it has come from and where it is going—most days anyway. Malcolm's too. But we were not traumatized by the war and the discord it brings. Mary was, even though her maam and *daed* sent her to America to be safe. But at what cost to her tender spirit?"

"Refusing to discuss it afterward didn't help," Debbie added. "When she asked questions, they wouldn't answer, so they never healed her feelings of rejection. Her daughter and granddaughter weren't allowed to ask questions about their roots either. It was as if the past was shrouded in secrecy. Now it's coming back to haunt them."

"How sad that something done in goodness became a stumbling block." Mrs. Stutzman clasped her hands. "My family took folks in during the war. Some liked what we did. Some did not. We paid no mind, because we knew we were doing the right thing. But life here was different from life in Europe. Evil reigned there, sweeping from nation to nation and leaving madness and devastation in its wake. Who can blame a parent for saving a child?" She met Janet's gaze. "I did not know why Mary was upset. Bits, yes, but not all. One day she said that she had been a burden at home, a burden to her aunt, and another burden to her family here because she was a reminder, and her mother did not like reminders."

"Oh dear." Compassion flooded Janet. "She felt like an outsider, and yet I expect her parents were glad they'd had the foresight to send her to safety. A lot of children were sent to places of refuge during the war. Why did it affect Mary so much?"

Debbie said, "I expect it was the silence, the refusal to explain their decision."

"Ach, ja!" Mrs. Stutzman agreed. "Not talking about it, not explaining, keeping it quiet as if it was wrong. Or as if it was something to regret. How does a child understand such grown-up things?" She shook her head vigorously. "They do not. It ate her up inside because her *bruder*, her *schwester*, they knew their parents, knew their love, knew their lives. Not Mary. She lacked that in her heart, in her soul. And yet she lived a good, caring life."

"But resentful?" Janet asked.

"Mixed with peace," Mrs. Stutzman assured them. "You must not think that she was always angry or upset. She would push her emotions to one side and do her job well. Private tears, I expect, and then later—much later—she told me she had forgiven her parents. When I asked what helped her to do that, she gazed toward her son, Daniel, while he hunted for a treat in the candy aisle."

Understanding struck. "Of course."

"'I would do anything to keep him safe.' Those were her exact words. She spoke quietly. It was her way. 'How can I resent my mother and father for doing the same thing? I'm sorry I never had the chance to forgive them when they were here. Maybe they know. Maybe they don't. But I will leave the past in the past and raise my son not to get stuck in the past, but to move forward in all things.'"

"And now Mary's granddaughter doesn't understand her silence," Janet said. "She was never allowed to ask questions about her grandmother's past. Now we can tell her it was because her grandmother felt rejected by her parents. Feelings matter. I think that's something we can all understand."

Mrs. Stutzman held up one hand. "That was important, yes. But it was the lie of who she was, where she was from, that truly cut her. Denying her place in the world, her heritage. I think she would have forgiven her parents much sooner if they had told her about who they really were. I remember the day a woman came into the store and told her, 'I'm your cousin Ida, and your name is Marysia,' as if Mary should know her. That woman pried open a door her family had tried so hard to keep closed."

Her story coincided with Martin Janek's account of how his family had stumbled upon Annie's daughter, working at the store.

"She realized she was living a lie. The rest might have worked itself out if she had been told the truth."

"So why wasn't she?" Debbie wondered aloud. "Why the name change? The subterfuge? Was it the aftermath of war? Had they done something that forced them to go undercover?"

Mrs. Stutzman pushed off the arms of her chair and stood. "That is not an answer I have for you. But I do not believe Mary's parents were bad people. Scared, maybe, but not bad. Although I have no proof either way."

"We're glad to have your opinion," Janet said as she and Debbie got to their feet as well. "Thank you, Mrs. Stutzman. I'm so glad you were willing to talk with us."

"The Lord has seen fit to keep me here for eighty-seven years," she replied. "And although I like organizing things from both sides of that door"—she jutted her chin toward the door they'd come through—"I also like time to talk and knit with folks."

Two older women walked through the back door and hurried forward with an air of excitement. Each one clutched a fabric tote bag.

"Four o'clock, on the dot," the taller one sang out.

"Perfect timing," Mrs. Stutzman said.

It was, Janet decided. She and Debbie made their way to the door to let themselves out. Janet indicated the women with a nod. "Enjoy your friends and your projects. It's been a pleasure, Mrs. Stutzman. A true pleasure."

The sincerity of her words made the older woman smile as the door swung shut behind them.

Kielce, Poland
November 1943

Dearest Nessie, hello!

I'm not sure when you will get this, if you do at all, but I have just finished a project. If it arrives before a new winter sets in at your home, God's blessings will be known for sure.

I used to not mind winter. It was simply a part of life, but I mind it now because too much thinking time comes with it.

When Marysia was young, we would fill our days with lessons and enjoying all of nature's wonderment around us. Yes, even the snow! In a small child's eyes, the change of the seasons is an amazement. I would laugh at the joy in her expression, her laughter and smiles as we explored the changes together.

It was a good life, and while we hoped to be blessed with another child, it hasn't happened. Now, with Marysia off to get her education, it is lonely here, but my work keeps my hands busy. Our little garden offered good vegetables again this year. I was able to glean some before it was set upon by those in charge. They send in soldiers to take what has ripened, but they don't come into the house to see if I've taken any. They seem to understand that I need to eat too. Last year they cleaned out everything, as they had the year before. This year they are more compassionate, if I dare write as much. Perhaps because this fight lingers so long? A fight they thought would be over in days or weeks is now years in length. Of course, if one spreads oneself too thin, it is hard to achieve one's goals, and men in power are rarely satisfied.

My winter supplies are cut greatly, for there wasn't much time to ripen more food before a bitter cold swept in and killed the plants. Still, since I am usually alone here, I can get by on a simple diet. When Joseph is here, we celebrate with a true meal. How I anticipate and treasure those days!

The workers used our land for wheat again this year, but not the rich wheat we've grown in the past. This grew stalky and spindly. It did not have the healthy seed heads we harvested of old. The workers showed little interest in the planting last fall, and weeds sprang up with no one to pull them. Surely that lessened their crop, and it made me wonder if this is repeated through-out our once-rich land? The talk of Germans moving in to take over the farms is still nothing more than talk. I think so many are conscripted to service that plans for farming and harvest have taken a back seat.

I surmise this on my own because I dare not talk to anyone about matters of importance. People in need can be persuaded to evil acts in order to gain food or warmth or shelter. It is a raw existence, and so I say nothing. I do nothing of note in the town. I nod and keep my chin down. What keeps me going are the occasional visits from our precious girl. To see her grow so well is a true blessing. And so, like Mary of old, I take these things and ponder them in my heart.

Another winter looms. When I fear I cannot bear it, I see my daughter's face as we send her off to new adventures in learning. We are blessed to have family heading a school deeply south. Lisbon has stayed as neutral as any place can in this dire situation, and that gives me a measure of confidence whenever I put her on a train. I pray, and I put our girl in God's hands, for none can do better for her. The lack of communication makes me second-guess everything, and then I think of Him, and the cross, and all that was given up for me, and I go on as I know I must—trusting.

I pray this gets to you, dear Nessie!

God's blessings to you and yours as you receive another gift of my hands.

God be with you.

Anya

CHAPTER NINETEEN

They didn't have time to browse the entire store, but they did do some pantry shopping before they crossed the parking lot to Debbie's car. She'd just started the ignition when a tap on the passenger-side window made them both jump.

Janet rolled it down quickly to speak to Mrs. Stutzman. "Yes?"

The older woman leaned in, her brow furrowed. "I had a thought about Mary's aunt. The one that moved away. You know her?"

"Ernestine," Janet replied. "We know *of* her. She kept Mary until her parents came over after the war, correct?"

"That was the intent, I believe, but it sounded as if she was not one to show much kindness." Her expression showed her opinion of the suggestion. "Mary did not say much, but she did say she did not mind leaving her aunt's house. In fact, one time Mary said it was a dark cloud in her life to which she never wished to return. I remember being unsure what to say to that, and all I managed was, 'That is what it is like to be away from your maam and daed when you are small.' Then Mary said that was bad enough, but if they had known how her aunt had treated her, they would have felt awful."

"She never told them?" Janet asked.

"Not that I am aware of. But that could be why she felt lonely for so long. She had secrets of her own, and the whole family had more secrets. Secrets isolate. No one dared open the topics. She did not want to hurt their feelings, they did not want to talk, and the whole thing grew bigger because everyone held their tongues." She took a quick step back. "Gert and Birdie are waiting. I must go." She hurried away, moving swiftly for a woman her age.

Janet turned to Debbie. "I wasn't expecting that."

"Me either," Debbie replied. "But it makes sense. So much hidden for so many reasons, and all because they tried to protect each other."

"But at a significant cost to their relationship, strangely enough."

Debbie tapped the steering wheel as they reached a stoplight outside of town. The light turned green as Janet's phone pinged a text. She glanced down, then drew a deep breath. "It seems our anonymous emailer has arrived."

Debbie gasped. "Here in Dennison?"

"Close by." Janet read Sadie's text out loud. "'The phantom email person is here. I got a message that said it's time to end the silence. She's in the area and is going to drop by.'"

She'd barely finished reading it when her phone rang with a call from Sadie. She swiped to answer it. "Hi Sadie, we got your message and—"

Their friend skipped the usual greetings. "Okay, I'm trying not to freak out, but the emailer is here. Or close to here, and it's unnerving. I have no idea if this person means me harm, which may mean my girls are in danger. Should I send them to their aunt's place to keep them safe? Drew is overnight in Cleveland at a conference, so he's unavailable. Oh, why did I post that stupid doll?"

"Because it was a cool find and relatable to your online follow-ers. Take a deep breath. It's going to be okay." Janet's reasonable tone seemed to help, because when Sadie replied, she was calmer.

But not by much. "I don't want to scare the girls, and they never have sleepovers on school nights, but what if this person isn't some innocuous blast from the past? 'Time to end the silence'? Is that a threat or a promise? I have no idea, but I could kick myself right now." She took another deep breath and managed to get herself under control. "I started this whole investigation because I didn't want some embarrassing fact uncovered that would affect my chil-dren. But now I might have put them in harm's way, which is so much worse. What was I thinking?"

Janet wasn't nearly as concerned. "I have it on good authority that most hardened criminals don't follow doll repair shops on social media," she assured their friend. "But we'll loop Ian in to be on the safe side. And a person with bad intentions doesn't usually announce their arrival."

"That's a valid point," Sadie said. "And it wasn't as if this person was here last week to leave the notes or steal the doll, right? That we know of, anyway. So I guess I'm overreacting. I don't understand how Martin and Gigi and the doll and this mystery person fit together."

"I don't understand it either," Janet admitted. "We do seem to have a lot of things that aren't sliding into place. Sadie, is your home address online?"

"Isn't everyone's?"

"True," Debbie said. "Do you want us to come over?"

"No." Sadie sighed. "We're fine. I'm going to wait and see what happens when they reach out again. If he or she calls and wants to meet, can I set it up for tomorrow after the café closes? Assuming they don't find me overnight, that is."

"I can stay the night with you," Debbie offered.

"Or Ian can come and do a stakeout," Janet added. "I want you to feel safe."

"The thought of having the house staked out doesn't make me feel safe," Sadie said. "It makes me feel paranoid. No, I'm fine. We're fine. I'll keep the phone next to the bed, set to dial 911. Did you all learn anything from Mrs. Stutzman?"

"We found out your grandmother was a wonderful person with a big heart and a rough history," Janet told her.

"I look forward to hearing all about it." A young voice called out from somewhere in the Flaherty house. "Gotta go. Bria needs to be at practice for the spring concert in ten minutes. I'll see you guys tomorrow. And thank you."

"Our pleasure." They hung up, and Janet said to Debbie, "I won't be able to live with myself if we don't send Ian over and something happens to any of them."

"Agreed. I'm useless at subterfuge, but I do play a mean game of rummy. In this case, Ian will probably be better."

Janet called Ian and explained the situation.

He agreed with her that caution was called for. "I'll send Allen over there shortly, and then I'll cover the overnight myself. How does that sound?"

"It sounds like I married the best man in the world," Janet told him. "And you didn't even get mad at me for getting you into this."

He laughed. "Well, the day isn't over, lass. See you at home, and then I'll head back out."

That was exactly what he did.

Five minutes after he was gone, Laddie jumped up, went to the side door leading to the porch, and growled.

Laddie never growled. It wasn't in his nature.

Janet had been running through some spring baking ideas at the table, but she stopped and took in her dog. Laddie stood with his feet braced, tail up, and ears cocked. The little dog growled again. And somehow the soft growl was scarier than a big dog's growl, because Laddie was a friend to everyone.

But right here, right now, the little fellow wasn't a friend to whatever was on the other side of the door.

Instantly, Janet was grateful for a cop husband who'd installed excellent dead bolts years ago.

She didn't dare get up and switch off the lights to see outside. That would make her a target, revealing her awareness of someone else's presence when they were trying to go unnoticed.

But sitting in full view of the side window wasn't exactly a great option either. She slid to the floor, silent and cautious.

Laddie growled again, deep and low. He braced himself, ready to pounce.

A shiver raced up Janet's spine, and the hairs on the back of her neck stood up.

Who was out there? And why? A normal person would ring the bell or knock. Announce their arrival somehow.

It suddenly occurred to her that Ian's cruiser was usually in the driveway. Her best protection wasn't there, a telltale sign for anyone who might mean her harm. Had she and Ian put all that effort into keeping Sadie safe and not thought about themselves? Not realized that someone might be angry with her and Debbie for helping Sadie?

And how could all of this be about an old rag doll?

The dog gave a warning bark, loud enough to stir Ranger from slumber, but, being a cat, he went right back to sleep.

Laddie's ears perked up, and then he breathed softly, almost a sigh of relief.

He relaxed his stance then sat, eyeing the door with a quizzical tilt to his head. A moment later her little protector padded across the floor to her. He licked her face in reassurance.

"Please tell me it was a stray cat coming around to say hi to Ranger," she whispered to him. "Or maybe a stray dog scavenging a meal. I'd even be happy with that pesky squirrel that thinks our bird feeder is his personal buffet. Anything but someone seeking my demise."

The little dog seemed to like that she was on his level. He licked her again, happy to have a playmate, then pouted when she scrambled up and hurried to look outside.

She peered through the window and saw nothing.

The motion detector lights hadn't come on, so what good were they if people and animals could slip past them? That would be the first question she'd pose to Ian tomorrow.

She twisted the lock and pulled the door open.

No one was there.

No one was on the street. No cars, no people, no movement.

That didn't mean Laddie had given a false alarm. She knew better than that. Anyone could have darted through the few yards leading to the less-traveled end of Welch Street. There wasn't much more than trees, empty lots, and more trees, but the route offered ample places to park a car with no one noticing.

As if in confirmation, a car engine started up the road, beyond the trees. The engine wasn't loud, but the silence of the spring night made it seem that way. It drove away from where she stood on the steps leading to the sidewalk.

And then all was quiet again.

A part of her wanted to explore the outside of the house.

Another part urged her to run back inside and shut the door.

She ignored the latter and hurried down the steps and around the corner.

And there it was, duct-taped to the side of the house.

Another note, similar to the last ones and fastened to the corner of her house for all to see. *The doll is where it should be. Stop searching for it. Listening to liars and cheats comes to no good—not for you or for them. Take heed.*

She didn't touch it. She went back inside, driven by determination and fury. She grabbed a pair of latex gloves, slipped them on, and hurried back to the corner of the house. She took the note down carefully, brought it inside, and slid it into a small bag for safekeeping. Then she locked the door and fumed. Bad enough someone was pestering her and Debbie at work or at Sadie's. But at her home? Where she lived with her family? That was going too far.

She made a video conference call to Ian and Debbie. "Someone was here. Our anonymous note writer has struck again, warning us to avoid cheats and liars."

"At the house?" Janet was pretty sure she felt the heat behind Ian's words through the phone by the way he snapped those three words. "Just now?"

"Don't worry. They're gone. Laddie went into protector mode when he heard someone outside. They taped a note to the side of the house using plain old silver duct tape. When I opened the door—"

"When you *what*?" Ian yelped. "Please tell me you didn't do that. Please tell me you didn't open the door, ready to confront whoever might be there."

"Well of course I didn't do it while they were here." She rolled her eyes at him. "I waited until Laddie relaxed. And they were long gone, but I heard a car start up and leave, so I'm guessing they parked on the upper end of Welch and walked here, then ran back there. It would have been about the right length of time. But of course, I didn't see it."

"So we're still being warned off." Debbie tapped a finger against her chin. "But we know that the email person wasn't here to leave the other notes—according to them, at least—and we've eliminated Martin Janek."

"Which leaves us at square one," Janet said.

"What about Sadie's neighbors near the doll hospital?" Debbie asked. "She said that some of them were annoyed that she inherited the building and the business and Estelle got nothing."

"That's worth examining," Janet murmured thoughtfully.

"I should come home," Ian said.

"No, you stay there," Janet insisted. "If they meant me harm, they wouldn't have run away. I'm fine, and I'm going to bed so I can be at my best tomorrow. Hopefully we'll get to meet Sadie's email author and see if we can put a piece or two in place that way."

"I want to be at that meeting," Ian insisted. "I'm not keen on my wife and her best friend walking into a dangerous situation."

"I appreciate that," Janet said. "Nothing like a big ol' armed cop to make a person want to reveal confidential information, right?" His frown indicated that he understood her point, but he wasn't happy about it. "We'll see what happens in the morning. I bagged the note. Probably nothing on the paper, but you might be able to lift a print or two from the tape. That stuff is always getting stuck on itself when you're working with it, and the person might have been careless."

"I'll check it out, but that only works if the person is in the system," he reminded her.

"I'd actually be happier if he or she weren't a career criminal," she remarked. Then she yawned. "I'm out, guys. I wanted to keep you updated. And yes, everything is locked, and the alarm is set."

"We don't have an alarm," Ian said, sounding puzzled.

Janet aimed the camera at Laddie. "Oh yes, we do. And he was on the job tonight. See you both in the morning."

As she hung up, she hoped she could convince herself that she was as unconcerned as she had acted.

Kielce, Poland
March 1944

Dear Nessie,

A fever runs through the town. The whole town, it seems. Many are sick, often with tragic results.

We are quarantined as much as we can be, which means no supplies come this way. The trains roll through without stopping. Even Joseph cannot pause here and leave a small meal or check on his sick wife.

I thought I was getting better at one point. I felt a thread of energy. It waned quickly as the fever took hold once more.

I ran out of water with no energy to get more. I kept dreaming of Joseph, of Marysia, of running through the wheat with you, and it was as if I saw our beloved Frank standing on the edge of the field. He beckoned me but then stopped beckoning. He raised a hand as if to stop me from coming, but even as he did that, he faded from sight.

Such a vivid dream.

I woke up to fresh water near the bed. A full bucket! And clean rags to bathe my face, my forehead, my neck.

I did not pause to ask who brought the water. Who risked illness and even possible death to be so kind.

It was life-giving water, the gift profound.

That was six weeks ago. A blink of time that seems like a lifetime, really.

I am well now. I was exhausted for weeks. The cold and damp and lack of food wears one down, but as the sun rose brighter and higher in the sky, so did my health, and finally, Joseph was allowed to stop here in town.

It was a beautiful reunion.

I could see he was scared. Frightened for me, for what had happened, and for how he was forbidden to check on me. He felt so helpless.

But God prevailed, and my health has returned.

I long for fresh food, but for now I get by, and Joseph does as well. We expect a late-term visit from our beautiful child once again. It is a brief stop, but welcome nonetheless. I save an egg each day to serve when she is here. And I have put away a small can of flour to make bread. With wheat crops gone to weed, flour is scarce and expensive. My own stores ran out long ago, but I had the wheat seed we'd saved from our final harvest, expecting to plant it again. With a small grinder I can work it into a fine, nutty-style flour. Not smooth like big wheels could turn, but ground enough to make griddle cakes.

She loves her visits home but knows her education means a great deal to her father and me. And she appreciates the safety of her school walls, although I take nothing for granted these days.

Her health and safety mean everything to us, and we will do all we can to ensure it. She is our blessing. If not seeing her often is the price I pay for her safety, I pay it willingly, if not happily.

I was nearly done with a lovely shawl for you when sickness took hold. I will send it when it is complete. It is pieced with trimmings of a fine dress and cape I made for a captain's wife. I used a deep red for the trim—ruby red, a rich tone that sets off the softer colors and brings out the splash of dark red in the floral squares within.

The captain's wife is coming today for a final fitting. I must tidy up a bit. That does not mean what it used to mean, dear Nessie. Naught gets out of place, for there is no one here to mess things up.

Everything is in its place, all the time. Once I would have been happy about that, but not in these circumstances.

It is not the existence I expected, always longing as I did for a house full of children.

I pray the war ends soon.

I pray for your family's safety and prosperity.

I pray for peace and the safe return of my beloved husband.

Ever yours,

Anya

From the Diary of Anya Oleski

Poland
March 1944

She knows.

The Nazi captain's wife. She knows.

Fear grips my heart, and terror grips my soul.

She told me today that she brought the water to me when I was sick. "I couldn't leave you to die here, alone," she whispered, although no one was around. "I had to do something to help. I know of your work." She spoke softly. So softly. "You talked about it in the delirium of your fever. I know what you are doing. I wish I had the courage to do the same. Not all think as I do," she went on. She speaks a broken combination of Polish and German, clear enough for us to communicate. She has acted as interpreter for two of the other women.

"But they also don't see as I do, or think as I do," she continued. "No mother would have her child return to this even once or twice a year if they were living safely elsewhere. No one will ever know of this from me," she promised. The sincerity of her voice and her

words was supposed to put me at ease, but all I could think of was Joseph.

How the soldiers would come and take us and execute us as they've done to others. All because of me. All this time, I have been scared and resigned and scared again, but today it isn't fear.

Today it is sheer terror.

She leaned closer. "War never lasts forever. Someday, this will be done. Some things will go in your favor, but do not trust time to mend things." She spoke as if she knew things I didn't. "Go when you can. Take the first opportunity to get free. Russia did not take kindly to my country chasing them out of here. They are anxious to swoop in to keep whatever they have gained and take more. Tyrants." She whispered the word.

I couldn't help thinking Russia wasn't the only country it applied to.

"We are in a time ruled by tyrants," she amended, "and I pray each day for God to remove them from power. To bring peace. My husband did not imagine this when he became a soldier fifteen years ago." She shuddered and seemed to be honestly sharing her feelings.

I pray she is not merely a convincing actress.

"He thought of border patrols and keeping things calm. Running a unit, something he does well." She scanned the walls of my little room. "And now this— an invasion against innocent people, a war, and then more wars in so many places. I believe it will end soon, Anya. Surely it must." Compassion filled her gaze.

And yet my heart raced at the very idea that some- one knew what we had done and are still doing. She holds our lives in her hands, and there is nothing I can do about it. I, who have helped others, am helpless.

Then she said, "The more I pray, the more I believe He will do as I ask. I hope you can soon reunite with the ones of your heart, Anya. You are surrounded by armies that mean harm. I pray that no harm ever comes to you or yours."

Tears filled my eyes.

I couldn't stop them. She handed me a handker- chief from the bag she carried. Then she pressed her payment into my hand, took her order, and left.

I am still shaking so hard I can barely write.

Inside and out, I tremble with fear such as I've never known. All this time believing we are so clever, so strong—yet the mere thought that she knows, that anyone knows of our deception, has filled me with dread.

Stand with me, Lord. And may legions of angels, saints, and martyrs join me in prayer for the end of war.

Stark fear fills me because another beloved is scheduled to come home again next week.

And I cannot explain how absolutely terrified I am.

CHAPTER TWENTY

Janet double-checked the locks before she went to bed, but she wasn't scared. Unnerved at most. The more she thought about it, the more the threatening notes felt minor-league rather than from someone who knew what they were doing.

Even so, she found herself scrutinizing her windshield as she approached her car in the predawn gloom the next morning.

No note.

Debbie had just joined her at the café when Ian called Janet. "I'm heading your way in fifteen minutes. I might have found something on a neighbor's doorbell camera last night."

"That's great." Janet slid two trays of their signature chocolate chip cookies into the oven. "Hurry over. Coffee's on."

It was still dark when he arrived. Daylight saving time had erased the early sliver of light she'd grown accustomed to, but they'd get that back as spring progressed. Ian parked in the lot, close to the road, and strolled across the street, as rugged and handsome as the day she'd married him.

"Hey, Chief."

He gave her a crooked grin then waved Debbie over. "Check this out."

They leaned in to see the video on his phone. The camera was angled enough to catch a white car making a left turn.

Janet frowned. "What are we seeing?"

"A car heading away from our area about three minutes after you heard the engine start up."

"Really? And you think this could be the car? But how did you get this when you were over at Sadie's?"

"Pastor Nick's niece lives over that way. I called and asked if she caught any activity coming from the east on her camera, and she did. That was the only car that came from that direction around that time."

"Can you read the license plate?" Janet asked.

"Nope. We'll see if we can get it cleaned up, but the angle is off so it might not do us any good. Someone else might have a better shot. I can get an officer to go around to the rest of the neighbors later today."

Janet turned to Debbie. "Do you recognize the car?"

Debbie shook her head. "I wish I did. It's nothing special, no markings and not distinctive. It could be any white car."

Ian picked up his coffee. "I've got to get over to the station, but I wanted you all to see this first."

"Thank you, honey." Janet reached up and kissed him. "Nothing weird or odd reported from Sadie's place last night?"

"Not a peep."

"Then I'm back to baking."

"And I'm prepping bacon," Debbie added, but once Ian had left, she glanced around. "Why do I feel like we're in the middle of a Venn diagram? You know the thing where circles intersect, and they have that shared part in the middle? We have three circles—Martin

Janek, our anonymous emailer, and a person leaving threatening notes. And right smack-dab in the middle of their intersection is that doll. Somehow."

"I feel the same way," Janet answered. "I keep wondering what we're missing, what we're overlooking. Nothing fits together."

"Maybe they don't," Debbie said as they walked into the kitchen. She got the bacon out of the fridge.

"Then we've been spinning our wheels. And we're no closer to any answers." Janet measured some flour into a bowl. "We often end up solving puzzles by finding that last piece that brings everything together. I'm hoping the anonymous email person gives us something to go on—and that the storm heading in this direction tracks north. I'd like some nice weather for once. March has been a bear so far."

Debbie chuckled. "It's certainly come in like a lion, but I haven't seen a single sign of the lamb yet."

Janet texted Sadie, but when Sadie texted back, Janet resumed mixing her dough. "Sadie hasn't heard anything. She's working at the shop, and she has the door locked so she can see anyone who wants to come in before she opens it. That makes sense."

Debbie adjusted the heat beneath the big griddle. "Better safe than sorry." She laid out the bacon, and Janet heard it sizzle. Debbie would cook it till it was nearly done and then take it off the heat so that Janet could finish off the pieces one order at a time. Their breakfast sandwiches on a grilled hard roll had become a popular phone-in order, and bacon seemed to be the meat of choice lately.

"Have her call us as soon as she hears anything, okay?" Debbie asked. "We can be done here by two forty-five. I'm anxious to hear and see what this person has to say. Hopefully they're legitimate.

You know how old mysteries tend to bring all kinds of con artists out of the woodwork."

Janet sent Sadie the message, and when Sadie sent back a thumbs-up emoji, Janet put her phone on the counter and got back to work.

A few hours later her phone buzzed with a call from Sadie. She washed her hands and answered the call.

"I've heard from M.E.!" Sadie exclaimed.

Janet picked up her friend's train of thought quickly. "The mysterious emailer called?"

"Yes," Sadie said. "Five minutes ago. It's a woman, so Debbie was right."

"A point she'll no doubt love," Janet said. "We better not wax on about that and risk her getting a big head. Perish the thought."

Sadie laughed, but it was a nervous laugh. "She wants to meet with me at three o'clock. I said we could, but it has to be at a neutral place, like a coffee shop, and you and Debbie have to be there. She didn't seem to have a problem with that, but then I heard there's a storm coming that could cause power outages, so I wasn't sure where we could meet. If that storm hits hard and businesses lose power, they'll shut down. Then what?"

The threatening weather could certainly be a factor in where they met. "Good question," Janet replied. "Normally I'd suggest meeting here at the café, but the floor waxers are coming in this afternoon. That means it'll be very noisy and not private, so we don't want to meet here. The good news is I saw a weather update a few minutes ago. The storm isn't supposed to last long."

"Well, that storm has left a few thousand people without power a couple hours west of here," Sadie said. "Maybe it would be better to meet at the doll hospital after all. There aren't any big trees near the house."

Sadie was right. Much as Janet wasn't thrilled about an unknown person with unknown intent being on their home turf, the storm changed everything. That's My Baby was likely the safest option after all.

"That sounds good," Janet told her. "If the storm gets here around midafternoon like they say, it's better if we're at the doll shop. Then if we lose power, it's no big deal. We'll have hours of daylight, even with a storm. I've got orders coming in, so I need to go. See you at three, okay? Hopefully a little before then."

They were about to close when Janet's father walked into the café. He waited until Janet finished ringing up the last customer then stepped forward. He held out a white waxed bag, the kind that bakeries had used for decades. The bag was yellowed with age, and the top was folded neatly. It was pressed into a flat shape.

"What's this?" Janet asked.

Paulette moved closer. So did Debbie, wiping her hands on a towel.

"It was in that little dresser," Dad told them. "Tiffany called me because the bottom drawer wouldn't close right. I noticed right away that the outside of the drawer was deeper than the inside."

"A false bottom," Janet said.

"That's exactly what it was," he confirmed. "There was a tiny spring latch at the back of the drawer. It was corroded with age and took a while to open, but when I did, the bottom of the drawer lifted out, and I found this inside." He unfolded the top of the bag, and the women peeked in.

"Letters," Debbie said.

Janet was dying to drop everything and read them, but they needed to get started on cleanup so Paulette could go home and they could go to the doll hospital on time. The letters would have to wait. "We'll check them out later," she said, although every fiber of her being shouted at her to see what was in that bag. How long had the letters been in that dresser? And whose letters were they?

"I'll stay," Paulette told them. She kept her navy blue apron in place. A cheerful train engine and railroad cars splashed notes of color across the dark background. It was one of Paulette's favorite aprons, and it suited her well. "You get into these letters. I'll start sweeping the floor."

"Are you sure?" Janet asked. Paulette was kindness itself, and Janet didn't want to take advantage of her generous nature. "You stayed overtime last week, remember?"

"I do," Paulette said with a chuckle. "And if you remember, I said I didn't mind at all, and I still don't. I'd much rather be here eavesdropping on you all and your shenanigans than sitting at home waiting for some game show to come on."

Janet laughed. "I don't believe you're quite that unoccupied, but in this case, I'll gladly take you up on your offer. I can't wait to see what's in this bag."

Paulette moved toward the kitchen. "Take your time. And be sure to speak loudly." She laughed and disappeared through the door.

Janet, her dad, and Debbie sat down at a table near the counter.

Janet lifted the cache of papers out of the bag. Some of them were in envelopes, but not all. She handed one stack to Debbie and another to her father and kept the bottom one for herself.

"This one is from Annie to her sister, Nessie," Debbie said. She held up her first sheet. It was clear it had been folded at one time. Faint crease lines were visible, evenly spaced, and then another fold to lessen the paper's width.

Janet scanned her first letter. "So is this one."

"Any mention of Mary?" Debbie asked.

"Not that I can see," Janet answered, disappointed. "Nothing personal, really. Just sweet letters. Sending blankets or something like that, things she made. Letting Nessie know to expect them."

Dad lifted his second sheet. "This isn't a letter. It's more like a diary or journal, like the one your mother keeps." He squinted at the page, and his eyes widened. "Annie Harper wasn't shipping blankets to America. She was shipping children!"

"What?" Janet took the paper and held it out so Debbie could read along with her. The journal entry was dated March 1944.

> Knowing we've been found out leaves me in terror. I can't sleep. I cannot so much as meet Joseph's eye, much less tell him that the captain's wife knows. How he will fear for me. Not himself. Never himself. But if he is afraid for me, then he cannot do his job. And if he cannot do his job, they'll send us off like so many others. I must keep up the charade. I must mend and sew gowns for the ladies while my husband keeps the train going.
>
> There is so little left here. I don't know what will happen. I've sent Nessie news of each arrival, and I pray that she meets them with open arms and finds a safe haven for each one. She placed her trust in me with the farm and the jewels left from

our beloveds. I trust her to take care of the children, each little Marysia I've sent into her care.

I pray for the girls whose names are written in my heart. Amanda. Eloisa. Dorothea. Martina. Esther.

I pray every day, hoping my prayers are heard, hoping that what I'm doing by working for the wives of the German soldiers isn't the gravest of sins. That grace may be found for me, for doing what I must to survive so that I may continue the real work. And I pray that each little girl arrives in a new land, ready for a fresh start, safe and sound.

I get no word from Nessie, but I put my faith in God and Him alone.

Yet it is a hard act, and despite the captain's wife's promise of secrecy, my heart quakes in fear.

I cannot speak to the rightness or wrongness of what I'm doing, what we're doing to stay alive in these times, but I know God will sort that out in His way, His time.

If we get out of this—if we move to a new land, a new opportunity, a new place with our beloved daughter—I have sworn to keep this veil of secrecy. The long arm of the Nazis respects no border or shore, and I have no desire to be hunted down. As much as it will pain me, I will not even be able to let Lester and Ida know where we are. It is better they think us dead than put these precious girls and our own beloved Marysia in danger. Only Nessie and George will know the truth.

May God bless me for the good I've done and forgive me for helping the enemy.

Blessed be His holy name.

CHAPTER TWENTY-ONE

*J*anet stared at Debbie.

Debbie stared right back.

Dad broke the silence. "They risked their lives to send children to safety."

"What an incredible act of courage," Janet whispered, even though no one was around to hear. It seemed like the kind of thing that should be spoken of in reverent tones. She shifted through her papers. "I have two reports of shipped goods here."

"And I have two," her father reported.

"And I believe I have the first one, dated in 1939. The one that was sent to let Nessie and George know Mary was coming," Debbie said.

"Unbelievable." Janet's hands shook. Her heart felt a little shaky too. "The thought that they risked death and probably torture to do this amazes me. The family lived here for years, with no one knowing a thing, thinking they were all dead. And then..."

"And then Martin's grandmother saw Mary." Debbie's voice shook.

"And his grandfather, knowing absolutely nothing about how his relatives had saved children, came to Dennison and accused them of stealing all those jewels."

Her father appeared a little bewildered at her words, so Janet started at the beginning and told him about Sadie finding the doll and posting it to her website, the anonymous email, finding the brooch, and Martin's visit.

"How did Annie and Joe respond when Martin's grandfather accused them?" Dad asked.

Janet scrolled through the notes on her phone. "Here it is. Annie and Joe told Martin's grandfather that the jewels had been 'put to a good use.' They insisted they didn't steal them."

"Do you think they used them for the girls?" asked her dad.

Janet lifted her shoulders. "Smuggling children doesn't come free, right? And what better use could the jewels be used for?"

"What I don't understand," Debbie said, "is if the doll was used to help children escape from the dangers of war, why are people upset? Why is some woman sending Sadie emails threatening to break her silence and let the truth be known? Why is someone leaving anonymous notes on our cars and at your house, warning us to stop searching for the doll and stop associating with Sadie?"

Janet's dad crossed his arms and gave her the same look he used to give her when she was a teenager withholding information about where she'd been and what she'd been doing. "Care to elaborate on these anonymous notes for me?"

"You don't need to worry, Dad." Janet sent Debbie a pointed glance then smiled sweetly at her father. "Ian knows all about it and is concerned enough for the both of you. Besides, the notes really aren't all that threatening."

Her dad uncrossed his arms and sighed. "I guess if Ian is on the case, I can rest easy. But I'd like to be kept in the loop if there are any more, okay?"

Janet squeezed his arm. "I promise."

He patted her hand. "So what about these emails? You know it's a woman now, right?"

"Yes, and she's in the area," she told him. "We're supposed to meet with her and Sadie around three to find out why she emailed Sadie about the rag doll."

"Those emails didn't say anything overtly threatening, did they?" her dad asked.

"The emails were cryptic, so they could be read either way." Debbie tapped the arm of her chair with one finger. "She used an anonymous email with a no-reply address and the initials M.E. She said things like 'the time for secrets is past.'" Worry crossed her face. "What did she mean by that? And does she mean harm to Sadie?"

Her father's eyebrows rose. "And you think it's all right to meet with her? I'd pull Ian in on that meeting. Who knows what people are thinking these days? Did you research her on the internet?"

Janet was about to speak when a gust of wind roared in from the west. The depot's proximity to the broad stretch of tracks provided a wind tunnel effect. When storm fronts blew in, the depot stood solid, but they could hear the wind broadsiding the multiple train cars used by the museum. She stood. "Dad, can you help Paulette finish up and close things down? I want to head over to Sadie's right away and let her know what's going on. I'll call Ian too."

"I should go with you two," he said, but then he scanned the café. "But I'll stay and help here. You call Ian, and for heaven's sake, whatever you do, try to stay out of trouble, will you?"

"We will." They grabbed their jackets, purses, and the bag of letters, and hurried to Janet's car.

Normally, it was a quick drive to the doll hospital.

Janet couldn't imagine the email writer wishing Sadie harm, but seeing that doll on social media had stirred something in people. For whatever reason, it had inspired this woman to reach out.

Why anonymously?

What did she know?

And why did she feel the need to travel here from parts unknown to confront Sadie in the middle of a wretched storm?

Okay, that last was a little unfair. She probably hadn't planned the part about the storm.

The wind buffeted the car.

It bent tree limbs low then hurled them high. Smaller branches peppered the streets already. Nothing major, but enough to warn the locals that danger loomed.

Janet crossed over into Uhrichsville as another gust hit the car. She was about to make the turn toward the doll hospital when Debbie let out a little screech next to her.

"What?" She couldn't stop and look. Keeping the car on the road and heading straight commanded her full attention.

"Sadie sent a text." Debbie's voice caught. "It just says, 'Help!'"

Chills raced up Janet's spine. "That's all it says? Call her, Debbie. See what's going on."

"On it." The call crackled through the hands-free system then went straight to voice mail.

"Trying again." Debbie hit Sadie's number again with the same result. No ringing. No answer. Merely Sadie's voice mail message.

Janet groaned in a mixture of frustration and concern.

Debbie scowled at the phone. "What's happening? Why would she send that text and then not answer my call?"

"Try Ian," Janet said.

Debbie swiped the screen, and they waited, listening to the phone ring.

Janet groaned when she heard Ian's voice asking Debbie to leave a message.

Debbie gasped when That's My Baby came into view. The small parking area was empty, and Sadie's car was nowhere to be seen.

They parked and hurried to the front door. It was locked.

They cut through the garden area to get to the side door. Also locked.

The key under the decorative rock was missing. There was no way to get in. Was Sadie in there? And if not, why not? It was two forty-five. The meeting was scheduled for fifteen minutes from now.

"Do you think the woman came early?" Debbie had to shout the question over the wind.

"And kidnapped Sadie?" Janet led the way back to the car, and they climbed in.

The rising wind pummeled the car, but they didn't need to worry about that. There were no big trees on the property. Nothing to bring them harm at the moment.

But where was Sadie?

"Could she have gone home for something?" Janet wondered out loud.

"She'd have told us that, wouldn't she?" Debbie stared at her phone as if willing it to ring. "And she sent a cry for help."

It didn't make sense. Did the woman mean Sadie harm after all?

A car drove into the driveway, a young man behind the wheel. He pulled up to the left of them. An elderly woman rode shotgun in the passenger seat. She beamed at Janet.

Janet rolled down her window, and the woman did the same.

"Are you here to meet with Sadie?" Janet called.

"I am," she confirmed.

Janet had no doubt that she was speaking to the emailer, M.E. Which meant that wherever Sadie was, it wasn't with the mysterious emailer. M.E. was sitting in a car not six feet away.

And they had already determined that Martin Janek wasn't a threat.

So that left the anonymous note writer.

Janet stared around, trying to think.

That's My Baby was nestled in a nondescript neighborhood in an old section of town. The homes were well kept, but they weren't high-end. On the north end of town, where Sadie and Drew lived, the houses were newer and pricier. Not fancy, but inviting.

Her gaze settled on the old two-story on the opposite side of the street.

Estelle's house. Lena's friend. Lena's helper. Lena's close neighbor.

Like an old-school padlock, the tumblers began to click into place.

"I'm so glad you made it," Janet told the woman in the other car. "Could you wait here for us? We've got to run across the street. We won't be too long."

The woman nodded again, and both she and Janet quickly rolled up their windows.

Janet backed out of the driveway and pulled up in front of Estelle's house.

She hurried out of the car, and Debbie followed.

Estelle's garage was detached from the house and slightly behind it. Janet fought the wind to get to it. Putting two hands up to block the glare, she peered through the window.

A white car sat there, snug and warm, out of the cold and the wind.

She turned to Debbie. "Estelle's got a white car in there. It's identical to the one that security camera caught the night someone left a note on my house. Let's go see if Estelle has seen Sadie today. I think Estelle Parkins might have a little explaining to do."

They hurried to the front door. The wind fought them, but they persevered, and when they finally made it up the steps and ducked beneath the stoop's overhang, it was enough cover for them to catch their breath.

Janet stepped off the porch and crept to the front window. The curtains were drawn, but through the gap in the center she could see someone sitting in a chair. Someone who had the same hair color and build as Sadie. Was she tied to the chair? Was she really in danger?

Janet went back to the porch and relayed to Debbie what she'd seen.

"What are we going to do?" Debbie asked. Her hair was a tumbled mess, and Janet knew hers must be as well. "What's the plan?"

"I think we should go in," Janet said. "We don't want to give her any warning that we're onto her, right?"

"Shouldn't we try Ian again first?" Debbie held up her phone.

"Probably." Janet waited while Debbie swiped her screen and placed the call.

After a few seconds Debbie shook her head and typed on her phone. "Still going to voice mail. I'm texting him."

"In the meantime, it's up to us," Janet said. "What's Estelle going to do? Shoot us?"

"Probably not our biggest worry at the moment." Debbie tried the knob. "It's locked."

Just then, Janet noticed a very pretty rock in Estelle's side garden.

It was broad and slightly rounded, patterned with a lovely display of daffodils and jonquils on either side of the name PARKINS.

On a hunch she stepped down from the porch, rounded the decorative wrought iron fencing, and lifted the edge of the rock.

Estelle's spare key lay under the stone, like Lena's had.

She carried the key to the porch, breathed a prayer that Ian wouldn't arrest his own wife, and opened the front door.

She walked as quietly as she could farther into the entryway, and there, on the left, was Sadie, sitting calmly in a chair, eating a cookie.

Debbie had no qualms about making noise. "Sadie!" she yelled.

Sadie startled, and the cookie dropped to her lap. She waved at them and picked up her cookie, wiping the crumbs into her hand and calmly depositing them in her napkin.

Estelle was in the kitchen, her back to the door, shoulders shaking. When she heard Debbie, she whirled toward them, with something in her hands.

Despite her bravado of a minute ago, Janet almost expected to see a gun.

Instead, Estelle clutched two mugs. She faced them with red-rimmed eyes. Traces of tears stained her cheeks, leaving streaks in her carefully applied makeup.

"You've come to arrest me, I suppose." She handed a mug to Sadie then sat down hard in the chair next to her. "I deserve it. I know I do, breaking into the house like that, although I don't even think it can be called breaking in when one has a key, right?"

Janet exchanged a glance with Sadie. Then Debbie. Then Sadie again. "Sadie, are you all right?"

"I am. I told Estelle that I have a meeting at three, but I could see she was really upset. I didn't want to leave her alone in this condition." She grimaced. "Sorry about the text. I was half joking, and then my phone died, so I couldn't explain what was going on." She sent the elderly woman a compassionate smile. "I knew we couldn't miss the meeting, but it seems Estelle has a lot on her mind these days."

Sadie had mentioned before that Estelle had taken Lena's death hard. Janet couldn't imagine losing Debbie, and they hadn't been next-door-neighbor friends nearly as long as Lena and Estelle. She crossed the floor and took a seat next to the elderly woman. "Grief and anger can push us to do foolish things, Estelle. It's a rough com-bination, all told."

"But why was I so angry at my best friend?" Estelle's lower lip quivered. Her hands shook. When she went to set her cup on the coffee table, the shaking made the tea dance in the mug.

"Let me help." Debbie nestled the cup in her own hands and set it down. When Estelle thanked her, Debbie brushed it off with a wave of her hand. "We all need help now and again. That's what friends are for."

Her kindness inspired another round of tears.

Janet checked the clock. Five after three. "Estelle, would you mind if we held our meeting here? With you? You knew Lena better than anyone, so I think it would be good to bring you in on this. We're going to talk about the old doll that Sadie posted online."

"Even after I left you mean notes?"

Janet read the anguish in the distraught woman's face. "Even then. Would that be all right with you, Sadie?"

Sadie put her hand on Estelle's. "It would be fine with me."

"I'll be right back," Janet said. She pulled her jacket tighter as she headed outside.

CHAPTER TWENTY-TWO

"Is it all right with you two if we meet at the white house with the black shutters right over there?" Janet asked the occupants of the other car in Sadie's driveway.

The woman seemed fine with that suggestion, but the young man frowned in concern. "Why there?"

It was a fair question.

"Because the woman who lives there is a neighbor who was close to the Harper family. She's also been affected by the mystery and intrigue surrounding this doll and trunk. She's quite upset about it all, and I thought if we could sit down over a cup of coffee or tea, we could hear the whole story. Together."

"That sounds perfectly delightful and absolutely the right way to go about something like this." The elderly woman's voice charmed Janet with its lyrical tone. "I'm so glad the opportunity arose before the Good Lord called me home. It's one of those things that you mean to get to time and again, you know. Then something comes along and drives it out of your mind, but when I saw the picture of that doll, I knew." She bobbed her head, seemingly oblivious to the wind raging around them. "And here I am. Declan, you don't mind heading up the road a bit, do you?"

The young man eyed Janet, then the older woman, and smiled. "Anything for you, Grandma."

Janet led the way. Once they'd parked the cars, she ushered Declan and his grandmother to the front door.

Debbie swung it open. In Janet's short absence, they'd added a couple of folding chairs to the circle around the coffee table. In the center of the table sat the rag doll that had started the whole adventure.

As the three of them entered the cozy living room, Sadie took their jackets and hung them on an elegantly carved coat tree. Debbie filled a kettle and put it on the stove to boil.

The young man handed over a box of cookies. A box of cookies marked with the Whistle Stop Café logo.

Janet took the cookies, surprised. "That's our place, you know." She exchanged a smile with him. "The Whistle Stop Café at the depot. Were you there this morning?"

"We stopped by the museum to pass some time right after it opened," his grandmother said. "I told my wonderful grandson that one should never go to an important meeting without something to offer the table. There was a rack of packaged cookies outside the ticket booth, and we grabbed two—one for now and one for the ride back. I hear they're very good."

"We hear good things about them," Janet said with a smile. "I would have gifted you some if I'd realized. You've come from wherever you live to help us answer questions, so cookies would be the least we could do."

"We're glad to do it." The young man put a hand on his grandmother's shoulder. "Do you want me to stay?"

She patted his hand. "Yes, dear. I want everyone to hear what I have to say." She took in the faces around the circle. "Not just you folks, but for future generations too." She faced Sadie. "I want Declan to hear this because if it hadn't been for your great-grandmother, I probably wouldn't be here today. Let's start with that and the five other girls who owed Anya and Joseph Oleski their lives. Beginning with your grandmother Mary, the *first* Marysia Oleski to be shipped to America."

CHAPTER TWENTY-THREE

*S*adie's mouth dropped open. "The first Marysia Oleski? There was more than one?" Disbelief colored her tone and expression.

Janet, who had read Anya's diary entry, wasn't as surprised, though she was still puzzled.

"Wait!" Debbie called from the kitchen as the kettle whistled. "Don't start until I get in there."

Janet chuckled. "Let's get settled, and Debbie will bring us some tea." She gestured to the coffee table, surrounded by five chairs.

Declan helped his grandmother into an armchair, and she sat back with a sigh. "I'm ready for a cup of tea and one of those delicious cookies."

Debbie brought in a tray with everything they needed for tea, and after a few minutes of small talk, stirring in sweetener, and exclaiming over the cookies, Sadie said, "I'm dying of curiosity. What did you mean when you said that my grandmother was the first Marysia Oleski to be shipped to America?"

"There were six," the woman replied. "Beginning with your grandmother—the real Marysia. But we should begin with introductions, of course. I'm Eloisa Cadwallader. Cadwallader is my married name. My maiden name was Grazcek. I was the third girl to be sent over and one of two still alive." She handed Sadie a sheet of paper. "Here are the names, ages, and whereabouts of the other women. I've included short bios like family details, as well as where the ones who have passed on are buried. Your great-grandparents were caught between the proverbial rock and a hard place. The Nazis needed Joseph's help with the trains. They kept him on to continue his route. It seems he had an amazing talent for engines."

"We heard that same thing from our former stationmaster," Janet said. "She made him sound like he was in a league of his own when it came to trains."

"An accurate statement." Eloisa folded her hands, and her gaze grew contemplative. "But while Joseph was running trains, Anya was caught in the middle of the Nazi occupation. According to my daughter June, who has done some in-depth research on this subject, Anya was a seamstress for the wives of the Nazi officers occupying their town. She made dresses and mended their clothes and their children's clothes. She served the enemy by day and rescued children by night."

"Oh, Gigi," Sadie whispered.

Eloisa smiled at her. "As I said, there were six of us, including your grandmother. And we were all referred to as Marysia until we were safely in America. That's where the M.E. on my emails came from. I was Marysia Eloisa."

"I'm sorry. I never knew anything about all of this, so I never would have put that together," Sadie confessed.

"It's quite all right, dear. Now, six may not sound like a great accomplishment compared to others who rescued hundreds, but what Anya and Joseph were willing and able to do made all the difference to us. They sent their daughter to America when she was five years old. They pretended she'd gone off to an English school in Lisbon, as Anya and her sister had when they were children. In reality, Marysia came over here to live with Ernestine, Anya's sister. Then, one by one, Ernestine's husband met five other little girls at the New York harbor and brought them to live with families who were willing to take them in."

"Did these girls have parents like Joseph and Anya?" Sadie asked. "Were they waiting at the end of the war to reunite with their children?"

Eloisa's smile grew sad. "Not all of them. I've been in touch with the other girls and know their stories. My parents, and the parents of two of the others, were killed before we came here. The families we went to adopted us."

"How did they do it?" Debbie asked. "Living with the enemy so close, working for them every day—how in the world did they manage to do this right under the Nazis' noses?"

"Martina's mother, Julia, said it was Anya's greatest passion," Eloisa said. "Martina was the fourth girl. The fourth 'Mary.' Her parents came over on the same boat as Anya and Joseph, so there was time to talk. I met Julia about forty years ago when I tracked down all the girls. Anya told Julia that she lived in fear of being discovered, even on the boat. She said she and Joseph had to make some sacrifices, but she was glad they'd done it because she couldn't have lived with herself otherwise."

Sadie reached out and grasped Eloisa's hand. "They never spoke of such things. To anyone. None of us had any idea."

Eloisa set her teacup on the table. "How could they speak of it? They lived through the atrocities of the Nazi invasion. They saw their friends and neighbors lose their lives, their homes, hopes, and dignity. They weren't wrong to fear the enemy's long arm of retribution, for us as well as for themselves and their family. You must remember—Joseph and Anya had gone through two heinous wars and a Great Depression. Like many folks who found their way to freedom, they merely wanted to move on. Live their lives. Not look back."

"I think that's exactly what they did," said Sadie. "They didn't look back, and they didn't let anyone else look back either. Did you know they changed their names from Joseph and Anya Oleski to Joe and Annie Harper?"

"I knew they changed their names, but I didn't know what they changed them to. Anya told Julia on the boat that they were going to do that. She said if the Nazis came searching for Anya Janek Oleski, they would never find her, because she no longer existed. They didn't stay in touch with anyone once they got to America—except of course, her sister," Eloisa told them. "Anya wanted privacy. As far as I know, she was able to melt into life here. At least, none of us girls ever found her."

"Do you know anything about her sister?" Janet asked. "Besides the fact that Mary lived with her?"

"I know she and George lived in New York, and they came to meet the boat that Anya and Joseph were on. They brought Marysia with them. Julia told me it was not a happy meeting. She didn't know what happened, but Ernestine stormed away and left Anya in tears. She said Ernestine's husband was very upset that his wife had acted that way and tried to comfort Anya."

"My great-uncle George," Sadie said.

"Yes. Julia wasn't close enough to hear anything. She said Anya seemed desperate to try to make Ernestine understand something, but apparently, she wasn't successful. That's all I know. I'm sorry it's not much."

"You've told us so much more than we knew," Sadie assured her. "I'm so grateful to you for coming all this way to share the story." Tears sparkled in her eyes. "To know they did such a thing is amazing, something our family can be proud of. I'm humbled and delighted that you reached out to me."

"I simply had to when I saw the doll," Eloisa replied. She gently picked up the doll, running fond fingers over it. "Imagine my surprise. I saw this doll, and it was as if the Holy Spirit Himself spoke to me and told me it was time to end the silence. You see, we each had a rag doll exactly like it. Anya used scraps of material leftover from her work for the Nazi officers' wives to make them. A doll so ordinary and worthless that a soldier would think nothing of it if he glanced our way, and certainly nothing anyone would bother stealing from a child."

"But why?" Sadie asked.

Eloisa took a sip of her tea. "She was so clever. She sewed a piece of jewelry into each doll, meant to help pay for the girls' lives in America. She believed that if her family knew the truth, they would value the lives saved by the jewelry. Julia said Anya told her that children were far more precious than jewels. That they were the jewels of God's kingdom. We were told to never let the dolls out of our sight and to give them to our foster parents right away. I remember when I gave my doll to my new father." She chuckled. "You should have seen his face when I told him he had to rip it open. He couldn't believe I was serious. When he saw the necklace inside, I thought his eyes would pop out of his head."

"Well, now we know how the doll ended up in a trunk in Lena's attic," said Janet. She turned to Eloisa. "Annie inherited the trunk when Ernestine died. Annie came to live with Lena, and when Lena died, everything went to Sadie."

Sadie leaned forward in her chair. "You said something in your email about potential and freedom within the doll. That's what made me look inside and find the brooch. I'm sorry if you felt I was disrespectful with the doll, posting it where anyone could see."

Eloisa ducked her head, and her soft cheeks grew pink. "No, no, I'm the one who should apologize to you. You had no way of knowing what that doll meant to me. To all of us."

"So is the doll I found the one Mary had?" Sadie asked.

"And if so, why was the brooch still in the doll?" Janet added.

"Yes, it's the doll Mary had," Eloisa replied. "I don't know the answer about why the brooch was still inside, but I can guess. She was little, you see. Younger than the rest, and how does a little one barely ready for school keep everything straight? Did she forget, perhaps? Or maybe her aunt never got the message to check inside the doll."

"There's something else that has me puzzled," Janet said. "How did Anya choose which girls to send? Did she know your families? Were you all from the same town?"

"Ah, I haven't told you why we were the fortunate ones." Eloisa's eyes brightened, and she sat up a little straighter. "You see, Anya had a clever plan. She told people that she sent Marysia to an English academy in Lisbon, when she had actually sent her to America."

"That's what Martin told us," Sadie said, gesturing to Janet and Debbie. "He's a relative who found me—also from when I posted the doll. His grandfather was Anya's first cousin."

"I'd love to meet him sometime," Eloisa said.

"I would be happy to arrange that," Sadie told her.

"I look forward to it." Eloisa nodded. "As I said, the real Marysia was the first to be sent, in 1939. Then Poland was invaded. Five times over the next five years, Anya welcomed 'Marysia' home for the holidays. Of course, it wasn't the real Marysia. Every year, Joseph, who traveled all over on the train, would search for a girl who resembled Marysia—well, resembled how she might appear as she was growing. He needed to find a girl who was the same age Marysia would be that particular year."

"Clever, though it sounds tricky, since he didn't have his own daughter as reference," Debbie murmured.

"It was indeed. So the rest of us were older when we made our journeys over." Eloisa counted off on her fingers. "Amanda was six, I was seven, Dorothea and Martina were both eight, and Esther was ten. I didn't know it then, but I know now how blessed I was to have the right features and be the right age in 1941."

Janet sat back, amazed. "Of course, that must be the explanation for why the brooch was still in the doll." She and Debbie exchanged glances. "Mary was likely too young to remember what she was supposed to do. And I bet she got attached to the doll. No five-year-old girl is going to voluntarily hand over her beloved doll for someone to rip up, even if it was to her extended family."

"And the other five of us went to loving families," Eloisa said. "We went to people who had volunteered to take us—who wanted us. Your grandmother went to someone who hadn't asked for her and who apparently made it abundantly clear that she wasn't welcome. How sad is it that the one child who went to her own family had the toughest experience? If the scene on the docks was any indication, her life couldn't have been very happy with them, and I for one am not surprised at all that she didn't give up the one thing she had that reminded her of home and a mother and father who loved her."

Mrs. Stutzman had mentioned something similar, how living with Aunt Nessie hadn't been easy on Sadie's grandmother.

"Do you think it was a money situation?" Sadie asked. "Being strapped for cash, perhaps? Would that have made Ernestine resent having to take care of Mary?"

"But if that was true, then Annie would have told Ernestine that she *did* send money in the form of the brooch, and that misunderstanding would have been cleared up, right?" Debbie glanced between Janet and Sadie, eyebrows raised. "The only conclusion I can come to is that they didn't talk about money or the brooch or anything like that. That's why the brooch was still in the doll. Ernestine didn't know it was there, and Anya assumed Ernestine had found it and made use of it to provide for Mary."

"Then maybe she was upset about Annie using the jewels without the family's permission," Sadie suggested.

"Wait!" Janet's exclamation pulled all eyes to her. She felt a thrill of excitement. "Ernestine and George met the Oleskis at the dock in New York City. They brought Mary to be reunited with her parents. So now Ernestine knows that they're in the States."

She gazed around the circle and saw blank expressions.

"Don't you see?" Janet said. "Anya—now Annie—must have told her that she and Joseph—now Joe—had decided not to contact the rest of the family to let them know they were there. We know from what Martin said that the family never heard from Anya and Joseph after the war ended, so the belief was that they'd died of illness or were killed by the Nazis."

"Okay," Sadie said, but Janet could tell her point hadn't landed yet.

She leaned forward and spoke with emphasis. "Ernestine knew the truth and kept their secret. For years she stood by, silent, while her family mourned Anya's and Joseph's deaths. Imagine what that must have done to her."

Debbie's eyes widened. "There's even more to it than that. This is all so complicated. Do you remember? Martin said the family believed that Mary was in school in Lisbon, when all the time she was with Ernestine and George in New York. So it wasn't the first secret Anya had asked Ernestine to keep."

Janet locked eyes with Debbie then patted the paper sack on her lap. "We might have some answers here." She handed the bag to Sadie. "Dad found this when he was working on the dresser you gave Tiffany. He found a false bottom in a drawer, and this was inside. It's full of letters, notes, and what seem to be diary entries from your great-grandmother. We haven't had time to read all of them, but we skimmed enough to know she was an amazing woman. And that she had good reason to fear for her life. She might not have shared those reasons with anyone else, but she was wise to keep her silence. And what a legacy this is to share with your two girls," she added.

Estelle had been distraught when they'd walked in the house and found Sadie. Now she shook her head through her tears, and her expression was one of wonder. "I was trying to find the brooch," she said. "The one that caused trouble between me and Sadie. The brooch that was meant to care for Mary when she arrived in the States all those years ago."

Janet stared between Estelle and Sadie. "Trouble between you and Sadie?"

Sadie took the older woman's hand. "Aunt Lena promised the brooch to Estelle."

"Goodness," Debbie said quietly.

"That's why Estelle left the notes and let herself into the house to take the doll," Sadie continued. "But of course there was nothing in it, because we found the brooch first and gave it to Ian for safekeeping."

"Lena knew about the brooch?" Janet turned to Estelle. "How?"

Estelle pursed her lips and then took a deep breath. "Mary told her about it. She never did confess to her parents that she didn't give the doll to her aunt Ernestine when she arrived. Or that she'd misplaced it a couple of years later—in that heirloom trunk, apparently. Lena told me the story during one of our winter's day tea sessions a few years back. She said as far as she knew no one had found the doll, but if she ever did find it and the brooch was still inside, she would give it to me for being such a good friend for so long. Folks around here thought she should leave the business to me, but they were wrong." Estelle blotted her eyes. The tears had finally ground to a halt. "What would an old woman like me do with another old woman's business? I can't give it the energy it deserves."

Sadie patted Estelle's arm, earning herself a watery smile.

"I knew the doll hospital should be left right where it is, in Sadie's hands. But I loved my friend Lena, so when Sadie posted the doll picture, I went a little crazy. Not for the doll necessarily." She swallowed hard. "Or the jewel inside. I couldn't stand watching Lena's things be tossed to the curb or put into a dumpster and carted away." She put her hand over Sadie's. "I knew the place needed to be cleaned out, but it broke my heart to see it, and I reacted angrily instead of simply talking to you. I hope you'll forgive me. All of you." She included Janet and Debbie in her woeful expression. "I'm so very sorry for leaving you those notes. And I'll gladly give back the doll."

"And I'll give you the brooch, as promised," Sadie told her. When Estelle began to shake her head, Sadie's tone grew firm. "I will, and then what you do with it is up to you. Aunt Lena meant for you to have it, and it was hers to give, if it was ever found, so all's well. And now"—she redirected her attention to Eloisa and Declan— "we know so much more of the story. Why they hid, why they stayed silent, and why things went as they did. It is an absolute blessing to know that I come from people of such faith, courage, and conviction. Thank you, Eloisa, for making the trip down here."

Eloisa dimpled. "It was my pleasure and God's timing." Then she yawned, and her shoulders slumped.

Declan took the hint. He stood. "Gram, we should be getting on, don't you think? It's a five-hour drive back to New York."

"Will the storm make it difficult?" Janet asked.

Declan shook his head. "We'll be fine once we get down the road. Gram never sleeps well in strange beds."

"We have that in common." Estelle held out a hand to Eloisa. "It was a pleasure to meet you. I can't even tell you how much it means. And how your story blessed me."

Eloisa made the round of goodbyes. She took a few moments to use Estelle's bathroom, and while she was in there, Declan said, "Seeing that doll, getting this done, letting folks know what happened back then—it has all meant a great deal to her. Thank you for letting us visit."

"We appreciate so much her coming all this way," said Sadie. "The trip can't have been easy for her, and we're grateful to you for bringing her."

Janet thought of something she'd been meaning to ask. "But why the anonymous emails, Declan? Why no name?"

He chuckled. "Gram has a healthy distrust of technology. She's sure her computer is spying on her. If she goes on social media, she never uses her name or anything close to it. If she has to send an email that isn't to a trusted friend, she uses the secure account." He shrugged into his coat. "Fortunately, you're squarely on the trusted list now, and she'll write to you from her regular account."

Sadie walked Declan and Eloisa to the door. She waved as they drove away, then wrapped her arms around her middle and joined them around the coffee table again. "I'm flabbergasted. Never in my wildest imaginings did I think of something so amazingly selfless and wonderful when I wondered about our family's odd reluctance to discuss our past. I'm so glad to know the truth now. And knowing what I know, I won't keep it a secret any longer."

"Oh?" Janet asked.

Sadie lifted her chin. "I want the world to know what Anya and Joseph Oleski did. Not for myself. For them. Because there are six women who got to live their lives in a free land because of them—to say nothing of the girls' descendants. And what a marvelous thing that is."

From the Diary of Anya Oleski
Dennison, Ohio
October 1946

I have stayed away from writing for some time.

My heart and head have not worked together since the war ended. They spin like the hands on a broken clock.

Joseph touches my hand and says, "This will pass, my love. It will pass." He said it there. He said it on the passage over. And he has said it here, in our new land, despite my sister's anger with me. An unjustified anger, it is, for how was I to know of her troubles here? Of her losses? There was no word, and so I wrote what I could and should, but she thought I was thrusting arrows into a grieving heart.

They remained in New York, she and George, but I do not think she will stay with him. He is a dear man, but her anger sears everything around her. I will pray for her constantly, for she was once such a source of inspiration for me. My heart aches that she has turned away, another casualty of war. To lose her children, Stefan and Audra, in a horrible car accident. What a tragedy. What heartache. I heard nothing of this because I received so few letters from Ernestine, even though she sent them regularly. What a terrible hardship on her and George, on their hearts. I can't imagine their pain. And to have me sending children— healthy, whole, and growing children—merely tore open the wound in her heart.

And again, my beloved pats my hand and says, "It will pass."

I thought him wrong. Then we learned that I was with child again at long last. A child to be born in time for Thanksgiving, a fine holiday here, and the blessing of the Lord's birth next month! We are elated. Somehow the knowledge that God has blessed us thus pushes old fears to the side in light of a new joy. I feel whole again, as if God and I have regained my heart and my soul.

We have adjusted our names so that they are untraceable, and that is how they will stay. My Mary is lovely. She did not know us at first. That scorched my heart, but she sees us as parents now. She doesn't know us, though, as her parents. Sending her on ahead was right in some ways and harsh in others, but she lives, and that was my goal. Everything else can be healed with faith, time, and caution.

We do not speak of the past.

It will never be forgotten. It cannot be. Horror is like that.

But it also won't be dwelt on or chattered about, because we have given enough time to matters of evil. Here, now, in this new and beautiful land, Joseph and I and our family will be what we yearned to be for long, harsh years—free Polish Americans, no matter what our name.

God be praised!

CHAPTER TWENTY-FOUR

he quaint dresser was completely refinished. Janet's dad had adjusted the bottom drawer slightly, leaving the historic hiding place intact but removing the finicky latch. He'd fastened a tiny leather lift strap in its place, leaving the drawers free to open and close as needed.

Ian placed it in Tiffany's room the following Saturday. He stepped back and smiled, but it seemed a little sad to Janet.

She looped her arm through his as she surveyed a room that had held so much of their life. So much of their love. "It went by fast, didn't it?"

He studied the room—the space that had been Tiffany's from birth—and sighed. "I never would have believed it, but yes." He jutted his chin toward the little dresser. "I'm still trying to wrap my head around how that's for her first apartment next fall."

"We have to make sure there are proper fire precautions in the apartment," she reminded him. "A fire escape if they're upstairs. Fire extinguishers and smoke alarms. And we'll make sure the windows aren't painted shut. You know what it's like when people renovate old places and make them into college rentals. We need to make it safe, okay?"

He planted a kiss on her forehead and smiled. "Will do. We'll give whatever they find a thorough going-over when they land on one, okay?"

"Yes." Her phone chimed a reminder. "Oops, we need to go. It's almost time to meet Greg and Debbie for our night out."

"Not *date night*?" he teased as she led the way downstairs.

"You and I can call it a date night," she assured him, laughing. "But we'll let Debbie and Greg come up with their own terminology. For now," she added with a grin.

Once they'd all been seated at the steakhouse, Greg brought up their most recent mystery. "How do you do it?" he asked once the waitress had filled their water glasses. "I get how people solve crimes that happen in the here and now." He poked Ian's arm. "You get to do that all the time, but something that happened eighty-odd years ago? How does one go about solving that?"

"God's guidance," said Debbie.

Janet nodded. "This mystery's been out there for decades, but until God's timing dropped all the tumblers into place, it remained unsolved. Sadie's inheritance, the doll, the trunk, cleaning out Lena's house, Lena's relationship with Estelle, and Eloisa and the other girls staying quiet all that time because Annie and Joe feared for their lives. I think all those things had to line up for everything to work out."

"And it did." Debbie lifted her glass of water in a toast. "To faith, courage, and conviction. The qualities that kept victims of war moving forward under hard choices and harsh conditions."

They clinked glasses and exchanged smiles.

"And Sadie gave her neighbor the brooch?" Ian asked.

"Two days ago," Janet told him. "All is forgiven. And Estelle is making the cutest doll clothes to sell at the shop. It gives her a little side income, and Sadie says the customers love it. They've already received over a dozen online orders, and more are coming in every day. All's well that ends well."

"And the Janeks are having Sadie's family over for Sunday dinner," Debbie added. "Another severed tie mended. Martin's family was stunned and delighted by Annie and Joe's story, and Martin's pastor asked him to share it with the congregation on Easter Sunday. Martin is thrilled to do it. It's too beautiful a heritage to keep hidden any longer."

Ian gave Greg a long-suffering expression. "I wish they weren't so good at this." He spoke in a wry tone, one brow up. "But as a guy who's had to pick clues apart to piece things together for over twenty years, I have to give credit where credit is due. You two are excellent at sleuthing, but under no circumstances are you allowed to put me out of my job. Is that clear?"

Janet laughed and touched his cheek. "Crystal clear. And thank you for the compliment, dear. That's really nice, coming from the local chief of police."

"And his friend." Greg raised his glass one more time. "To long-lasting friendship with the best people I know. Ian." He tipped his glass toward his lifelong friend. "Janet." He tipped it again, but when he got to Debbie, he didn't tip his glass. Instead, he put his other hand over hers. "And Debbie."

She blushed, but she didn't move her hand. Instead, she smiled up at him.

He smiled back.

And they stayed that way until the waitress began setting out cups of rich, beefy soup.

Janet exchanged a quick grin with Ian.

They deliberately didn't mention the shared moment, because Debbie and Greg were hardly high school sweethearts. They'd lived decades of life in different spheres. They both treaded carefully and quietly. They didn't necessarily have baggage. They had experience.

And if those experiences opened the door for something new and special together, Janet was all for it. But she'd keep her thoughts to herself for now, because if anyone deserved a chance at happiness, it was her best friend and Greg. She believed that with all her heart.

But she was mostly willing to let God sort that out because He knew best. On the other hand, if He opened the door for her assistance, well—

That was what friends were for, after all.

Dear Reader,

Dennison, Ohio, aka "Dreamsville," set the tone for a whole community of giving, sharing, loving, and helping as train after train of fresh-faced and not-so-fresh-faced soldiers, sailors, marines, and airmen rolled through on their way to deployment after the United States joined the Allied forces during World War II. Approximately four thousand people made it their pledge to provide a proper send-off for those brave men and women as their trains came through the Ohio depot.

I have always been fascinated by history and acts of heroism. The courage of armed forces in the face of danger amazes me. Bodies of military men and women, standing strong before an enemy, create an image of unity that cannot be dismissed. The strategies and the oversight a successful battle takes aren't simply in the hands of skilled generals. That success lies in the conviction and courage of every beating heart in the regiment or platoon or unit.

But it's the unseen courage of the behind-the-scenes people, the "everyday Joes" who risk life and limb to do the right thing, that inspired *That's My Baby*. This Whistle Stop Café mystery was inspired by the brave acts of Irena Sendler, Nicholas Winton, André and Magda Trocmé, André's cousin Daniel Trocmé, and so many others. The thought of their sacrifices and courage has inspired me to be a better person every day because they did what so many could or would not: they risked their lives for others.

I hope you love this story of how a past sacrifice created a future for a handful of people and how the effect of that trickled down on even our little town of Dennison, Ohio. It is my absolute pleasure to share this story with you.

Ruthy

ABOUT the AUTHOR

Bestselling, inspirational author Ruth Logan Herne has published over seventy novels and novellas. She is living her dream of being an author, and in her spare time she is co-owner of a rapidly growing pumpkin farm in Hilton, New York. She is the baker-in-residence, the official grower-of-the-mums, and a true people person, so filling her yard with hundreds of people every day throughout fall is just plain fun!

She loves God, her family, her country, dogs, coffee, and chocolate. The proud mother of six with a seventh daughter of her heart and fourteen grandkids, Ruthy lives in an atmosphere where all are welcome, no mess is too big it can't be cleaned up, and food is shared.

TRUTH BEHIND the FICTION

I mentioned in my letter to readers that I'm inspired by the stories of everyday folks who stand up to tyranny in their own way during times of oppression.

These acts of heroism aren't relegated to war alone, but in this case and in this time, the story of people like Irena Sendler encourage me to be a better, stronger person.

Irena Sendler was a twenty-nine-year-old Warsaw social worker when the Germans invaded Poland in 1939. Under the occupation, she worked to help Polish Jews in the "Ghetto," a cordoned-off area in Warsaw that quickly became overpopulated as regulations forced all Polish Jews to live there. Many of these were sent on to Treblinka as a way to alleviate the overcrowding. They were part of Hitler's final goal—the destruction of the Jewish people.

In 1943, Irena was named the Director of the Zegota Department for the Care of Jewish Children. This position offered her direct contact with multiple care homes and orphanages run by various religions. Using these contacts, she was able to save a great many children (some estimate up to two thousand five hundred), funneling them to places of safety. She was arrested in October of 1943 but managed to hide her records of children and their whereabouts before she was taken into custody, leaving no trail to follow. As with many underhanded ways of war, Irena's release several months later was the result of bribes to officials. She went into hiding, continuing her work, and stayed in Poland after the war.

She was awarded the auspicious "Righteous Among the Nations" award from Yad Vashem, the World Holocaust Remembrance Center, in 1965. She died in 2008 at the age of 98.

Even though tales of heroism aren't uncommon during war, each one should be remembered and celebrated.

JANEK
Family Tree

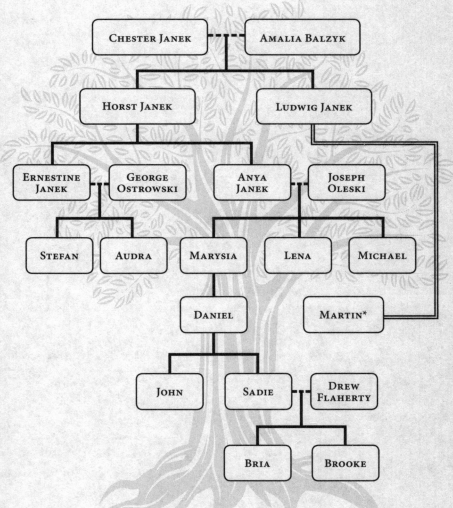

CHESTER JANEK - - - AMALIA BALZYK

HORST JANEK   LUDWIG JANEK

ERNESTINE JANEK — GEORGE OSTROWSKI   ANYA JANEK - - - JOSEPH OLESKI

STEFAN   AUDRA   MARYSIA   LENA   MICHAEL

DANIEL   MARTIN*

JOHN   SADIE - - - DREW FLAHERTY

BRIA   BROOKE

——— Janek Bloodline
- - - - - Marriage
═══ Generations in Between Not Shown

*Martin is Ludwig Janek's great-grandson

FROM the HOME-FRONT KITCHEN

Janet's Easter Bread

Easter breads are a long-standing tradition in many cultures, and the Polish versions are melt-in-your-mouth delicious.

Oddly enough, they're just like my husband's German grandmother's sweet bread. I love it when certain things cross cultures and folks recognize a good thing and share it!

Ingredients:

½ cup sugar

2 packages yeast

1 tablespoon vanilla extract

1 teaspoon salt

6½ cups flour

1½ cups whole or 2% milk

6 tablespoons butter, cubed

4 eggs (3 for recipe, one for glazing)

Directions:

Mix sugar, yeast, vanilla, salt, and 2 cups of flour in large mixing bowl. Heat milk and butter to about 120 to 130 degrees in saucepan on stove. Do not boil. Add milk mixture to flour mixture and blend. Add remaining flour and three eggs and mix thoroughly. If using a stand mixer, use a dough hook for this step. If kneading by hand, knead until smooth and elastic. The dough is ready when it cleans the sides of the bowl.

Grease or butter bowl. Put dough back into bowl, making sure all sides are lightly greased or buttered. Cover with towel and place in warm spot until dough doubles in size.

Preheat oven to 375 degrees.

Punch down dough.

Beat remaining egg with fork.

Separate dough into three equally sized balls.

Roll out each ball into a long rope about 1 to 1½ inches in diameter.

Lightly grease a baking pan or cookie sheet.

Braid the three ropes together on the cookie sheet. Form a circle, like a wreath.

Allow dough to rise once more, 15 to 20 minutes.

Brush dough with egg wash.

Bake at 375 until bread is delightfully golden.

May decorate with colored hard-boiled eggs, jelly beans, or coconut.

Serve warm or cold.

Read on for a sneak peek of another exciting book
in the Whistle Stop Café Mysteries *series!*

A STRING OF PEARLS

By Jenelle Hovde

Washington, DC
January 1, 1942

The phone rang, the sound jarring within the silent room. Jack Lund snatched the receiver from the telephone stand and pressed it against his ear.

"Hello," he said, glancing around out of habit to see if anyone might be listening. Gray light filtered through the curtains, barely illuminating his surroundings. The narrow hall and the shadowed kitchen remained silent and empty, despite the custard pie his elderly neighbor from apartment 11 had dropped off hours before. She had always insisted on feeding him, sharing what sugar she had, which was nice, since

there were rumors the president would ration sugar by the end of the month. Her matchmaking efforts to pair him with the local girls for a date, however, weren't as welcome.

"That you, Jack?" A deep baritone voice reverberated over the line.

"Yes," Jack answered, keeping it brief. His superior wasn't exactly a man who enjoyed social calls or chitchat.

"I want to go over the details of your vacation."

He grimaced as he shoved a hand into the pocket of his woolen pants. The ironing crease was much less crisp thanks to hours and hours of work. Victor Armstrong demanded the use of code words when speaking over the party lines, where strangers could eavesdrop. This was anything but a vacation. In fact, Jack couldn't quite remember a trip he'd dreaded more in his ten years working for the agency.

Regardless, he managed to infuse a touch of gaiety into his tone. "Of course. My baggage is ready. You remember Sam and George and all the gang, don't you? The ole boys are raring for a fresh adventure. There's something about those horse ranches and clear skies in California. They'll get a chance to pretend to be real cowboys for once in their lives."

A slight pause from Jack's superior. "Are you bringing Ricky? He's never left the city before. I'm worried about him."

Ricky. *Jack inhaled a deep gulp of air as his fingers entwined in the telephone cord. He had endured the grueling tests of West Point as a cadet, had broken an arm while scaling the white-capped mountains in Alaska, and had even run undercover to infiltrate the Italian mafia flaunting their business in New York. Now, he was on the cusp of one of the most significant missions of his life. It was situations like these that made a man's career—or broke it.*

Jack untangled his fingers from the telephone cord. "Ricky will leave with us this week. I didn't want to make him wait. There's too much angst with his mother at the moment for him to remain where he is."

A whoosh of air flooded the crackling line, as if someone had heaved a great sigh. It was the most emotion Jack had ever heard from his superior. "All right. Ricky will leave with you."

"I'll watch over him as if he were my brother." *Jack spoke the assurance, but his heart stuttered with an erratic rhythm. Right now, Ricky was hidden in a wooden crate no bigger than a standard trunk, crammed with other similar wooden boxes inside a* climate-controlled federal storage facility constantly guarded by none but the most trusted guards.

"I think you should travel light. Don't take the entire gang this time. And don't let Ricky out of your sight. He's a special kid who needs your full attention."

Jack closed his eyes for a moment as his mind made the rapid calculations of train schedules, stops, and final destinations. He had transported six similar boxes this past month. Arthur. Bill. Stephanie. Stephanie had proven to be quite a handful, requiring him to find an art expert and antique dealer who knew how to pack an elegant lady with care and discretion. Each box was labeled with a special name and assigned an innocuous spot in the train's baggage car.

But he had relied on his fellow agents to man the cars. A group of five of them met at the train station and discreetly took positions at the exits, monitoring the passengers, and then slipped onto the trains with newspapers pinned beneath arms and worn attaché cases in hand, as if on business.

It had worked so far with the last several train trips, one of which had led all the way to Fort Knox and underground bunkers tucked away in the most innocuous locations. Why was Victor wavering now? Had he received word of an internal threat? Was there a mole in the organization?

"My friends need to come with—"

"No, Jack. I've made up my mind. You travel with Ricky. Include Verne, if you must. Travel light and fast, with the cheapest luggage you can find—nothing too fancy for that rough country—and call me when you get to the ranch."

Victor's voice betrayed the slightest edge. Unusual for a man who had returned with white hair from the First World War and rose with distinction in Washington.

But Ricky—this package was the most important Jack had ever encountered. A cold sweat broke out between his shoulder blades. "Fine. But it's going to be an awfully lonely vacation."

A short chuckle burst from the other side of the line. "Maybe. Let's hope it's relaxing this time, old sport."

As abruptly as the phone call had begun, it ended with a sharp click, leaving Jack licking his dry lips. And then... a softer click, as if someone had heard all they wanted.

Blood thoroughly chilled, Jack hung up the phone. His fingers trembled as he rubbed his chest. His white dress shirt, rolled at the cuffs, was rumpled from hours of planning the so-called trip.

Was the listener merely another nosy neighbor, one of the retired ladies who asked him far too many questions in the downstairs lobby? Or, as Victor *feared, was it someone else? Since the Japanese had bombed Pearl Harbor and Germany continued to march deeper into Europe, everything had changed.*

Thank goodness for the code words. Mother, or the president of the United States, might not fully appreciate his new moniker, but it had proved to be an effective one. Only a handful of men knew what Jack was organizing and overseeing to the bitter end.

He dragged a hand down his face as he considered the train schedules departing the next day. He had more phone calls to make. Verne would be pleased to be included, but there would be plenty of other men who would be disappointed to miss the adventure of a lifetime, even if they didn't know what was in the boxes.

So much weighed on him that his gut ached.

One thing was for certain. He would never allow Ricky to fall into the wrong hands.

Debbie Albright slid her warm washcloth across the Whistle Stop Café counter where gobs of pink and yellow frosting puddled, and it wasn't yet ten in the morning. Her best friend and business partner,

Janet Shaw, had made fresh doughnuts, and that creamy frosting was a siren call to anyone facing another hectic Monday. In the café kitchen, Janet whistled along to Glenn Miller's "A String of Pearls" as it played softly over the radio.

The café had fallen relatively quiet following the early morning rush. An older couple chatted softly in a booth by a window framed with gingham-checked curtains. They shared a pot of breakfast tea and cranberry muffins.

Another woman waited at the counter, studying the chalkboard menu. She sniffed and dropped her gaze to the contents beneath the curved-glass display case. Wearing skinny jeans, a pair of rhinestone-studded boots, and a form-fitting cashmere sweater, she was quite dolled up this morning with artistic makeup, thick eyelashes, and long blond hair in loose but perfect waves.

"Anything calling to you, Gloria?"

Gloria Haverly ran the florist shop downtown. She was in her late thirties or early forties. Like Debbie, she had returned to Dennison to start a business, after working for an upscale boutique in California.

Gloria shook her head. "Do you have anything healthy, like oatmeal with almond milk and acai berries? Or kale and blue algae smoothies?"

Debbie bit the inside of her cheek to keep from laughing or saying something she might regret. She was pretty sure Janet would never allow algae and smoothies to go together. "I've got muffins, scones, and blueberry pie. Janet can whip up an omelet or a breakfast sandwich. She makes the omelets to order, with cheese, onions, ham, peppers, or anything else you have a hankering for."

Gloria grimaced as she tapped her nails on the glass—long nails exquisitely painted with miniature flowers beneath a veneer of gloss. "I suppose a scone will have to do. I really have no time to wait for an omelet."

"It's amazing, and hey, it's got fruit, right?" Debbie offered with a grin, but Gloria didn't smile back.

Resigned, Debbie pulled out a blueberry scone crusted with sugar. Janet didn't skimp on the blueberries, and she had perfected just the right blend of sweet and tart.

Debbie served the scone to Gloria, who didn't even bother to meet Debbie's eye or murmur a polite thank-you.

"Anything to drink?" Debbie prompted.

Gloria stared at the scone, poking at it with her fork as if it were a dead animal. "Tea, herbal. Do you have a blood orange breakfast blend?"

"You're in luck. We do."

As Debbie poured hot water into a teapot and arranged the teacup and spoon, she caught a glimpse of Gloria's face as the woman tasted the scone. Her expression betrayed pure bliss, if only for a split second.

Debbie set the teapot and cup and saucer on Gloria's table just as the bell over the café door jangled. Debbie raised her head and saw a familiar lanky form in blue jeans and a black T-shirt step inside. Greg Connor. Her pulse kicked up a notch as he ran his fingers over a stubborn cowlick. With thick, dark hair and brilliant blue eyes, he exuded a rugged charm.

"Hey, Debbie," he called out when he saw her, his expression brightening.

"Hey, yourself," Debbie answered, glad to see her friend.

Beside Debbie, Gloria straightened as she brushed aside her hair. "Why, it's Greg Connor. I haven't seen you in ages."

Greg cast Gloria a charming grin, as he did with everyone in town. "Nice to see you too, Gloria. I was glad to hear business has been good for you this spring."

"I had a rush at Valentine's Day. You should have seen the roses and carnations that went out to all the lucky ladies. But you know, Greg, I didn't see you in my shop for any red roses."

Greg coughed, his cheeks faintly pink. "Ah, well…"

Debbie cut in to rescue him. "Want some coffee, Greg? I've put a fresh pot on, although I'm afraid you've missed most of the dough-nuts after our latest morning dash. I have a few cake varieties left, but I sold everything else."

He nodded as he approached the counter. "Doughnuts and cof-fee sound great, but actually, I didn't come for that reason."

She set her tray on the counter, surprised. And maybe a bit con-cerned over his quiet declaration.

He blew out a long breath as he braced both hands on the counter. She noticed tiny flecks of white paint along his tanned knuckles. Nice hands. Strong and capable.

"You seem troubled. Anything I can do to help?" she offered. Their relationship, which had been one of the bright spots in her move back to Dennison after a stressful corporate job, had danced between friendship and something with the potential to be more.

"I actually came in to talk to you, if you have the time," Greg said.

"No problem." She nabbed two cream-colored ceramic mugs and poured the steaming hazelnut brew into both. A pair of glazed maple doughnuts were all that remained of the Monday madness. She slid them onto a plate and checked the clock. They had a few minutes before the lunch rush, and she needed a break.

Janet peered around the corner. She smiled a greeting. "Hey, Greg! Long time no see."

"Wanna join us for a coffee break?" Debbie asked the friend who had helped her fulfill a lifelong dream of running a café in the historic train station.

Janet arched an eyebrow. "I wouldn't mind a caffeine fix." She didn't bother to remove her apron, which covered a pink T-shirt printed with doughnuts.

From her booth, Gloria watched, a tiny frown lining her brow.

Debbie eased into the booth, delighted when Greg slid in beside her, a hint of his spicy cologne wafting toward her. Janet took the opposite bench, giving her a pointed grin, which Debbie ignored.

Greg cleared his throat. "I'm in somewhat of a pickle with the chamber. As you know, we couldn't have the Easter parade or egg hunt last month for the actual holiday due to awful weather. We've rescheduled the festivities for later this month, and I need some volunteers, if you'd be willing to pass the word around. Our parade organizer, Shirley Tussing, had to quit at the last minute. Her daughter is on bed rest with a tough pregnancy, and Shirley has basically moved into her house to help her full-time. No one else has stepped in to fill Shirley's shoes. No one decorates quite like Shirley. Her floats are famous around the area, so her absence leaves a big hole in our committee. We need someone to manage the meetings and oversee the floats, including the chamber of commerce float, and organize the Easter egg hunt after the parade for the kids."

Debbie heard a chair being dragged across the floor before she could register what was happening. She glanced up to see Gloria's wide eyes full of sympathy. "Oh, Greg, that's terrible news about Shirley. I want you to know I'd love to pitch in. Are you helping with the Easter parade this year?"

Of course Greg would be helping. He helped everyone.

Debbie pushed down her mounting frustration. She had no right to tell him who he could and couldn't talk to, but that didn't mean she didn't want to.

As Greg filled in the details of all that needed to be done and the hours spent working with him, Debbie's heart sank a little further. There was no denying the gleam in Gloria's calculating expression. She had to do something...

"I'll lead the committee, Greg," Debbie blurted out.

He frowned at her. "Are you sure? You're already so busy. I don't want you to burn out with everything you're juggling."

"It's no trouble. How hard can organizing a parade be? Most of the work is probably already done." She infused lightness into her tone, ignoring the sharp kick under the table from Janet. If Debbie's friend arched her eyebrows any higher, they would shoot right off her forehead.

Greg gently freed his arm from Gloria's grip. "That's great. Thanks, Debbie."

"You can sign me up too." Gloria smiled brightly. "A parade needs the expertise of a florist, and we'll make Dennison shine."

Debbie felt another shot of irritation, but when Greg placed a warm hand on her shoulder, she couldn't help but meet his smile with one of her own. "Thank you, Debbie. I owe you." Then he leaned down, making her heart flutter, and whispered in her ear, "I'm really looking forward to working with you."

He waved goodbye to everyone and thanked Gloria before exiting the café.

Debbie heaved a sigh of relief when a pouting Gloria finally left.

"I sure hope you know what you're doing," Janet muttered under her breath as Debbie cleared the plates from the table. "You can't help everybody. You've got to say no sometimes."

"It's fine. It'll get me out into the community and promote our business. That's a good thing, right? Besides, Greg must be worn out with all of his responsibilities and the boys."

It was an excellent reason to help, not that she needed the excuse.

A couple of hours later, Beatrice Morrow waited at the counter to pick up her take-out order of Denver sandwiches. Her usual sweet smile was nowhere in sight, her brow lined with a frown. She had retired from teaching elementary school after several decades, and Debbie had been one of her students. Today, Beatrice sported a pixie haircut and a sensible denim jacket against the April chill. She leaned over the counter, motioning Debbie to follow suit.

"Debbie, I desperately need your expert advice. It's urgent." Beatrice glanced around the restaurant, her eyes as wide as saucers, before lowering her voice to a stage whisper. "You remember when I told you my nephew came to town to crash for a few months and look for work? He found hidden treasure at my house, and now he won't stop digging in my backyard!"

A NOTE FROM the EDITORS

We hope you enjoyed another exciting volume in the Whistle Stop Café Mysteries series, published by Guideposts. For over seventy-five years, Guideposts, a nonprofit organization, has been driven by a vision of a world filled with hope. We aspire to be the voice of a trusted friend, a friend who makes you feel more hopeful and connected.

By making a purchase from Guideposts, you join our community in touching millions of lives, inspiring them to believe that all things are possible through faith, hope, and prayer. Your continued support allows us to provide uplifting resources to those in need. Whether through our communities, websites, apps, or publications, we inspire our audiences, bring them together, and comfort, uplift, entertain, and guide them. Visit us at guideposts.org to learn more.

We would love to hear from you. Write us at Guideposts, P.O. Box 5815, Harlan, Iowa 51593 or call us at (800) 932-2145. Did you love *That's My Baby*? Leave a review for this product on guideposts.org/shop. Your feedback helps others in our community find relevant products.

Find inspiration, find faith, find Guideposts.

Shop our best sellers and favorites at
guideposts.org/shop

Or scan the QR code to go directly to our Shop